Love's Endeavour, Love's Expense

The Response of Being to the Love of God

Love's Endeavour, Love's Expense

The Response of Being to the Love of God

WILLIAM HUBERT VANSTONE

Foreword by
H. A. WILLIAMS CR

Darton, Longman and Todd

First Published in Great Britain in 1977
by Darton, Longman and Todd Ltd
89 Lillie Road, London SW6 1UD

ISBN 0 232 51380 5

Printed in Great Britain by The Anchor Press Ltd
and bound by Wm. Brendon & Son Ltd,
both of Tiptree, Essex

Acknowledgement
The hymn by the author on page 119 is reproduced
by kind permission of James William Shore

To
Michael James Daman
cui amica veritas

CONTENTS

Foreword
by
H. A. Williams CR

Theological truth is the truth of God's relationship with man and it is the fruit not of learning but of experience. In this sense all theology, properly so called, is written in blood. It is an attempt to communicate what has been discovered at great cost in the deepest places of the heart – by sorrow and joy, frustration and fulfilment, defeat and victory, agony and ecstasy, tragedy and triumph. Theology, properly so called, is the record of a man's wrestling with God. Wounded in some way or other by the struggle the man will certainly be, but in the end he will obtain the blessing promised to those who endure.

The theologian in this respect is no different from the poet or dramatist. All of them must write in blood. Yet what the theologian is called upon to do with his experience is different from what the poet or dramatist does. Obviously it is different in form – the theologian *qua* theologian does not write poems or plays. His idiom is more abstract. He has to translate his experience into ideas and then arrange those ideas in as logically coherent a form as he can, so that reading his work is much more obviously a sustained intellectual effort than reading poetry appears to be or seeing a play. It is not, however, only in form or idiom that the theologian's work differs from that of poet or dramatist. Its centre of interest is always different and in two ways. First, the theologian's primary concern must always be God's relationship with man, and any relationship a man may have with his fellow-men or the world he lives in must always be subsumed under that primary relationship with God. Secondly, the theologian has been nurtured by a tradition of belief and practice and all the time he must relate his insights to the tradition which has nurtured him. However first-hand, and in that sense original, those insights may be, they cannot be entirely out of the blue. They have to connect in some way with insights already achieved.

What makes Mr Vanstone's book so remarkable is that it is the product of a theologian in all the senses described.

Nobody reading the book could doubt for a moment that it is the product of personal experience of a most costly and rewarding kind. On every page the book is alive with passion. We are given no theories but only truths which have been lived through and made the author's own. At the same time there is not the slightest hint of that self-indulgent exhibitionism which is the trap constantly laid for those who speak from the heart. What has been given by the heart is here intellectually disciplined and set at a distance so that it is rationally examined and evaluated by a mind which is exceptionally able and informed. Indeed the intellectual discipline has been so well applied that some will not find the book easy reading. That in places it requires from the reader an effort of concentration is a sign of its merit. We find the arguments expounded vividly enough if we are prepared to take a little trouble.

Mr Vanstone sees everything in the light of God's love for His creatures – a love which is not easy or imperturbably serene but which consists of a continual exercise of utmost effort, a self-emptying which gives to what it creates power over its Creator Who is for ever striving with every nerve to evoke the free response of love which He wants and indeed needs. Mr Vanstone has here seen the same vision as that given to some of the Christian mystics: that God needs our love as much as, if not more than, we need His. Mr Vanstone gives us an analysis of human love and leads us thereby to an apprehension of God's love. And in doing so brings vividly home to us what it means to speak of God's incarnation.

Yet the final result is nothing high-falutin. Mr Vanstone begins his book by introducing himself to us as a parish priest. And he presents the final outcome of his study as something which gives meaning and depth to the ordinary life of an ordinary parish church. He gives us theology as a reality to be lived both individually and corporately. He makes sense of the Church not merely as a grand idea but also as a building of bricks and mortar whose walls may need a coat of paint.

It is this combination of personal experience, intellectual discipline, deeply Christian concern, and insight into the significance of small practical matters which might otherwise be considered a nuisance which makes this book truly theological. It is, I believe, a masterpiece and will become a classic. And certainly it leads us out into the fresh air.

H. A. Williams CR

Introduction

This essay records an attempt which continued over a period of some twenty years to discover my own truth – to unfold or unravel a conviction which it would have been affectation to doubt and treachery to deny. The conviction was, and is, that the outward expression of religion, what Christians call 'the life of the Church', is a matter of supreme and unconditional importance. Being unable to doubt this conviction, I have attempted to discover what it implies.

Many people will not share this conviction. They will find it very easy to doubt or deny the importance of religion in general and, in particular, of such outward expression of religion as is observed and practised in the Christian Church. They may grant that my conviction is sincerely held, and that it is, in a sense, 'my truth'; but they will not recognise it as 'their truth'. They will find in themselves convictions as deeply held as mine but quite different from mine. My conviction will seem quite unconnected with, and irrelevant to, the convictions which give order and purpose to their own behaviour and their own lives.

But perhaps there is, all the same, a connection between their convictions and mine. Let us suppose that a blind man and a deaf man are together in a room when a thunderstorm breaks out close at hand. The blind man experiences and reports a loud noise; the deaf man experiences and reports a bright light; and each is convinced of the reality of his experience and the truth of his report.

But the two reports are different, and, on the face of it, that of which the blind man is convinced is different from that of which the deaf man is convinced. The 'truth' of one appears quite unconnected with, and irrelevant to, the 'truth' of the other. But if each should dis-cover his own truth, exploring the implications, the causes and the origins of that of which he is convinced, the two might soon recognise that what they had experienced in different ways and reported in different ways was, in fact, the same thing – the proximity of a thunderstorm. The 'truth' of each would then become relevant to, and even a confirmation of, the 'truth' of the other.

In a pluralist society the convictions by which the lives of individuals and groups are ordered often appear entirely disparate and unconnected. One person sacrifices his life in the cause of freedom. Another gives his life to the care of an invalid. A third spends his life in the study or preservation of some detail of the world of nature. A fourth confines his life within the austere walls and duties of a monastery. Each of these four would be called a person of strong convictions; yet the conviction of each appears unrelated to the conviction of any of the others. But if the conviction of each were explored and its implications detected and traced, it is possible that the four might be shown to have more in common than is at first apparent, and that mere mutual toleration might be raised to mutual understanding and enrichment. It is the purpose of this essay to show what is implied by the conviction of some people that the life of the Christian Church is a matter of great importance, and perhaps to win the understanding, or even the assent, of others who do not share this conviction.

The conviction with which the essay is concerned is by no means novel or remarkable. In substance it is scarcely more than a platitude, and it would not have seemed worthy of reflection or exploration but for the suddenness with which

it grasped me, illuminating and transforming circumstances in which personal anxiety was deepening into despair. First, therefore, I must explain these circumstances.
'Truth' says Tillich, 'is grasped in the Boundary situation': but truth so grasped cannot easily be shared except
with those who know, at least vicariously, something ot the
reality of the situation.

1. Autobiographical

My father, a clergyman of the Church of England, presided throughout my childhood over the same urban parish in the North of England. Both he and my mother were deeply absorbed in the life and work of the Church, and they allowed themselves, so far as I now recall, no other interest or pursuit except only the care and the well-being of their children. This second commitment of their life was largely bound up with the first. It was the evident belief of my parents that the good care of their children was among their most important duties as members and leaders of the Church; and, on the other hand, that the proper care of children included their training and involvement in the life of the Church. Therefore in both the duties and the pleasures of my childhood, home and Church were inextricably interwoven, and my memories of each are inseparable from my memories of the other. My share in the life of the Church was a natural extension of home-life; and the details of home-life, down to the time of meals and of going to bed, were largely determined by the activities and demands of the Church.

Growing up in this environment, I might have come either to love or to hate the Church: but I could hardly have come to regard it as a triviality. That the Church was a matter of importance was deeply imprinted upon my mind in my most impressionable years. A child will accept the importance of a custom, a person, or an institution long before he asks the reason for that importance: and so, no doubt, it was in my own case. But when eventually I came to ask this question, an answer lay ready to hand which was immediately satisfying and even appealing to a child. For the period was the depression of the early nineteen thirties, and the parish was one which included both an area of poverty and unemployment and an area of comparative prosperity. The two areas marched side by side; and it was precisely on the boundary between them that the Church stood. Its geographical position symbolised at least a part of its activity and importance: for through the Church, and stimulated by it, there passed a considerable traffic of concern and practical help from the one area to the other.

Of this traffic a child of the Vicarage could not be unaware. It was probably the major topic of my parents' conversation. My mother, a person of strong feelings and unsparing energy, would have heard of the distress of an individual or the plight of a family; and, having already done what she could, would spend a mealtime in pouring out suggestions of what more might be done, and in what way, and by whom. My father would listen with a judicious gravity which might have been mistaken for indifference: but often enough he would report, a few days or a few hours later, some step which he had taken or persuaded someone else to take. Memory suggests that this kind of conversation was an almost daily occurrence. Most commonly of course, it was material poverty which aroused my mother's indignation and my father's reflection: but sometimes the conversation turned on remedies for loneliness, for parental neglect or for lack of opportunity. The concern expressed in such conversation in the home was, as one might expect, echoed in and encouraged by my father's preaching in the Church. He taught that it was God's will that men should care for one another: and he represented the Church as the agent or instrument through which God's will should be carried out. No doubt he spoke also of many other matters:

but such is the dominant impression which remains with me of what he taught and of the direction in which he led.

I could not then, nor can I now, assess the volume of the traffic of kindness which passed through, and was stimulated by, my father's Church in those hard times. Measured against the need of the times it was probably small. But it was certainly greater than that which was stimulated and organised by any other voluntary agency of the district; and the spirit in which it flowed was very different from that which in those days animated the cold and meagre benefactions of the state. It was natural, therefore, that I should see the importance of the Church in terms of the effective kindness which it stimulated, directed and performed: and it was equally natural that, when the idealism of youth suggested that my own career should be one of 'service to people', the Church should appear the appropriate field for that career. I vividly recall, from my early teens, an incident through which my 'vocation' first became clear to me. An apple tree in the Vicarage garden bore a scant crop of which we were unreasonably proud. One day, seeing the branches of the tree shaken, I realised that the crop was being plundered; and I ran to protect it. The intruder also ran: but at the gate I caught him – a boy of about my own age. I grabbed at his arm to stop him: and I still remember the very thin wrist over which my hand closed. The boy wept; and said he was hungry; and pleaded with me to let him go. I let him go, saying nothing: but as I walked slowly back to the house the resolution formed in me that, if I could, I would follow my father's career. Given that I wanted to 'do something' about poverty and hunger, and given that the Church was what I believed it to be, my resolution was entirely appropriate.

This resolution was not seriously affected by the coming and passing of the second World War, or by my own experiences in the services and as an undergraduate. I sup-

pose that, like most of my contemporaries, I was aware that
society was changing, and that the acutely distressing
poverty of the early thirties was being alleviated if not
eliminated. But it was not clear that this change was
irreversible; and even if, for the moment, there was less
need to 'feed the hungry', there were many other social
needs which the practical kindness of the Church might
serve and meet. There was still a glaring contrast, for instance, between life at Oxford and life in the grimmer
streets of my father's parish: and though the undergraduate
left might argue that the remedy for this contrast lay in
political action rather than in such measures of alleviation
as the Church might perform, what the political left was
saying made no great appeal compared with what my
parents were doing. I remember that it was directly after a
political meeting at Oxford that I made the telephone call
which was decisive for my entry into the ordained ministry
of the Church.

My training for the ministry was helpful in many ways,
but it did not greatly affect my understanding of what the
Church was for, or of the reason for its importance. I still
saw it as the will of God that men should care for one
another, the more able for the less able, the more gifted for
the less gifted; and that they should do so not coldly or
arrogantly but with a deep sense of mutual belonging and
common brotherhood. I still saw the Church as the agency
through which this great and good cause should be advocated and advanced. During a period of study in New
York I came to see, through the influence of Reinhold
Niebuhr and Paul Tillich, the obstacles to the furtherance
of this cause which are present within the nature of man –
obstacles which do not disappear when man is influenced
by, or drawn into, the Church. I realised more clearly than
before the ambiguity of motive and the impropriety of
method which is present in the Church as in every institu-

tion. I realised that the Church itself might be partly to blame for those very ills which it was called upon to remedy. But the profound criticism which Niebuhr and Tillich levelled against the Church could be employed with equal or greater force against every other institution – political, social and religious: and it seemed improbable that other institutions, less given to such profound self-criticism, would better preserve their integrity and effectiveness. It still seemed to me that the Church, with all its faults, was the agency most likely to further the will of God by the practical promotion of the brotherhood of man.

I began my own ministry in another urban parish in the North which, in the thirties, must have been very similar to my father's parish. But my work soon brought home to me how far social change had gone. In parts of the parish poverty still existed: but it now appeared as a temporary misfortune rather than as a permanent condition. In the early nineteen fifties an atmosphere of social hope was present – an atmosphere created by a rising standard of living, new educational opportunities and the development of the welfare state. This last development was extremely important to anyone who reflected on the work and purpose of the Church: for it meant that there were now other agencies, with greater resources and perhaps with greater expertise, to do those very things which had been the daily concern of my parents and of my father's Church. Kindness such as my father had taught and practised was still possible, still useful and still appreciated. But it seemed less necessary: and one foresaw that, as the welfare state developed, it might scarcely be even possible. It would soon be anticipated and made obsolete by the almost automatic response of some agency of the state to any need or difficulty that might arise: and the brotherhood of man would soon be both achieved and expressed in the easy provision for all of those necessities of life which my parents had laboured so earnestly to supply to a few.

So the *raison d'être* of the Church, the purpose of its being and of its activity, seemed to be undermined. But I realised this only to realise that the Church in this district was fulfilling another and equally admirable purpose. It was maintaining and enriching the life of a community. In the new atmosphere of social hope people were looking for something more than the provision of the bare necessities of life: they were looking, in the modern cliché, for a richer quality of life. To a remarkable extent they were finding this richer quality through the Church and in association with the Church. In the centre of an area of small and closely packed houses stood the Church building, admirably maintained, surrounded by an attractive, open garden. Next to it were the two Church schools, equally well maintained. A stone's throw away was the sports field, the breathing space of the district, owned, supported and equipped entirely by the Church. In and around these three centres took place a rich and varied social life which grew ever more intense during the years in which I knew the parish. This social life involved, in one way or another, a very large number of people – certainly far more than were connected with any school or club or other centre in the neighbourhood: and it had been going on for something like three generations. In earlier times it had been a simpler form of social life: its facilities had been fewer, its camps and outings less far afield. But always it had been there: and out of it there had grown, in the course of three generations, a remarkable nexus of shared memories, local loyalties, long friendships and familial relationships. I discovered in this district what the word 'community' can mean: and I realised that, in fostering the sense of community and the reality of community, the Church had made, and was continuing to make, a rich contribution to the quality of many lives. The disappearance of the Church

from the district – a possibility which few were able to con-
template – would have greatly impoverished many people,
including many who would probably not have described
themselves as members of the Church.

I saw the worship of the Church as both expressing and
sustaining the life of the community. To a large number of
people it seemed entirely natural that, at least on the major
occasions of the year, they should come together in the
Church and thus, as it were, give outward articulation to
their unity of feeling and their mutual loyalty. It seemed
clear that it was this expression of community which prin-
cipally sustained community. For the people who came
most frequently to worship were also those who carried out
most diligently the practical tasks of teaching and visiting,
of leading and organising, which held the community
together. It was natural to suppose that what they heard
and did in worship was the inspiration of their diligence:
and it was reasonable to conclude that only this kind of inspiration – only the awareness, constantly awakened and
sustained in worship, of the nature and purpose of God –
could be adequate to support their labours and, through
their labours, the life of the community. It seemed to me
that the importance of the Church lay in the unique power
of its worship and teaching to sustain, among a a very large
number of people, the rich life of a happy community – a
community such as elsewhere I had never known.

There was, in fact, little time for this kind of reflection:
for, in such a community, there were endless and most
varied calls upon the time, energy and imagination of the
clergy – calls that gave to one a daily sense of purpose, a
frequent sense of achievement and an occasional and less
pardonable sense of one's own importance. I was grateful
for the support, the friendship and the confidence which
this parish gave to its clergy: and I was grateful for what it
taught them about the purpose of the Church in the new

society of the post-war world. Its purpose was to be the instrument of God's will no longer in the simple and appealing task of 'feeding the hungry' but in the complex but no less appealing task of creating and sustaining the life of a community.

I should have been glad to pursue this task in such a happy situation for a very long time. But after some four years I was informed by the Bishop that the time had come for me to undertake a new responsibility. I was to initiate the work of the Church in a new area of corporation housing on the edge of another industrial town some twenty miles away.

The Bishop explained the situation. There was, as yet, no 'presence' of the Church in the new area except a building in process of erection at the expense of the Diocese. No pastoral work had yet been started, no visiting done or enquiries made: no list was available of the names of people who might be interested or helpful: no house was available as my own residence. The building, adapted to serve for the time being as both a Church and a social hall, would be complete in some six months time: a part of it might then serve also as my own lodging. The Bishop suggested that, until it was complete, I should retain my present appointment but set aside a certain amount of time for visiting the new area, surveying its possibilities and forming my plans. At the end of six months I would have, in effect, a useful building, a reasonable sum of money – and a *carte blanche*.

My first visit to the new district was on a grey and bitter afternoon in January. There were few people to be seen in the streets and, of those to whom I spoke, none had heard of a building belonging to the Church of England. Eventually a man whom I questioned mentioned a half-finished 'canteen' on the far side of the estate. With some difficulty I found it: but when I went inside even the plasterers who were at work knew nothing of the ownership or purpose of the building. It was a label on a packing case, addressed to the Church of England Building, which confirmed that I had found the place I was looking for and the base of my future operations.

After this I was able to go across to the new district about once every ten days. Most of my time on these visits was occupied with the building itself – in inspecting the very adequate facilities which it afforded and in discussing the final details of their arrangement and decoration. But some time usually remained for walking round the district, for getting to know its geography, and for talking with anyone whom I met. I was dressed as a clergyman; and usually I explained that a Church was soon to be opened and that I was to be its Vicar. But not one person offered help, advice or support: in fact not one person expressed the slightest interest. Without exception people were courteous: without exception they were indifferent. I came to realise in later months and years that a good many people had in fact been aware of the coming of the Church and had been awaiting it with interest and eagerness: but it so happened that the paths of these people did not cross with mine. Between the months of January and May, in the course of more than a dozen visits to the new district, I met not a single person to whom the coming of the Church was a matter of any kind of personal interest. My inevitable impression was that people of this district did not want the Church.

One afternoon I made an appointment at the Town Hall and met a number of the civic officials who were responsible for the planning and supervision of the new district. It was the largest project of such a nature for which they had so far been responsible; and they spoke about it with pride and satisfaction. They told me that all was going well: that people had settled down happily in their new environment, and that already such amenities as a Community Association, a Dramatic Society and a Scout Group were in existence. They were aware of no social problems such as loneliness among the elderly or unruliness among the young: and they were confident that, if any such problems should arise, they could be handled within the institutions which were already in being or which were planned for the near future. Partly this optimistic assessment came from honest pride: partly, no doubt, it was kindly offered for my own encouragement. The speakers wished me to feel that I should be living in a happy and contented district. But the effect of their words was different. I was made to feel that the district had no need of a Church: it was getting on very well and very happily without one.

As winter gave place to spring, this impression was confirmed by my own eyes. There were more people to be seen now: and what I saw of their occupations gave the impression of nothing but innocent and harmonious contentment. The typical scene on a spring evening was of men working in their gardens and exchanging banter with their neighbours, while wives brought cups of tea or hung curtains and children played under their parents' eyes on the stretches of open grass in front of the houses. When I stopped to talk I was always received with easy friendliness: but there was never a suggestion that there was any need for a clergyman, or for a Church, in the district: no one spoke of problems in the home or with neighbours: no one sought advice: no one hinted that, as well as a pub and a few more shops, a Church might be necessary to the completeness of the district. In later months and years I came to realise that there were, and always had been, personal problems and unfulfilled needs in many people: but at the time these were not disclosed. The impression already formed in me was inevitably confirmed – that the people of the new district did not need the Church.

It may appear that it was naive of me to have trusted this impression and to have believed that any society could be free from the problems and the needs – social, psychological and spiritual – to which, traditionally, the Church has ministered. But it must be remembered that the period was the middle nineteen fifties – the period when the prophetic voice of Dietrich Bonhoeffer had already been heard in this country. Bonhoeffer had foreseen a post-war world in which man would have 'come of age', and in which he would be free from that *need* for religion which, in all previous ages, he had felt and recognised. Bonhoeffer believed that man was about to discover and display a new kind of strength and self-sufficiency: and he called the Church to recognise, accept and prepare for this new situation. He warned the Church against doubting the genuineness of the strength of the new society, against looking for, and hoping to expose, flaws and weaknesses in it. He taught that the Church would degrade itself if it sought a niche and field for its operations in the discovery of cracks and blemishes beneath the fair surface of the new society; he taught that the Church must learn to minister to man not in his weakness but in his strength. This phrase itself I found puzzling: for the word 'minister' seems to imply the existence of some kind of need – which the word 'strength' denies. But I accepted the general content of Bonhoeffer's prophecy: and it seemed to me that this new, post-war district was exactly the kind of place in which one might see it fulfilled. It seemed entirely possible that here, with no contribution by or from the Church, there might have been achieved already those goals of material well-being and of social, psy-chological and spiritual fulfillment, the attainment of which had been, in my past experience, the purpose and *raison d'être* of the Church.

Therefore it would have been improper of me to suspect what I had been told and what I had seen, and to doubt the happiness and self-sufficiency of this fragment of the new society. I felt that I must accept the evidence of my own ears and eyes; and that I must face the fact that, in my new situation, the Church would be neither wanted nor needed. It was extremely difficult to do so. I felt that, for the foreseeable future, my work would be no more than a formality, and my life a kind of charade. Perhaps some people would come together to form a Church; but they would do so of habit or courtesy rather than of need or conviction. Perhaps I should eventually find some satisfaction in my role as their Vicar: but it would be a satisfaction which I should not be able to justify. In truth, if and when the Church came into being, it would be a matter of no importance: its presence would make no significant difference to the district: its activity would be, at the best, a harmless hobby – an alternative to, and on a par with, the activities of the Dramatic Society and the Scout Group. It might have been easier to accept this future and this role if I had not still been engaged, between my visits to the new parish, in my work in the old parish. For there, as soon as I returned to it, work was waiting which clearly touched the depths of people's hearts and lives. People asked my help over matters that were important to them: they were deeply concerned that this or that should be done by or in the Church: and, knowing that I was soon to leave, they were the more open in speaking of what the Church meant to them and of any contribution that my own ministry had made. There was a painful contrast between the manifest importance of the Church in the one parish and its apparent triviality in the other: and it was in the other parish that my future lay.

Still, after more than twenty years, I recall very vividly how, between January and May, hope turned into apprehension, and apprehension into despair. I knew that I must accept my future, and tried to put a brave face upon it. But a coldness settled upon my feelings – a grim realisation that I was preparing not for a new kind of life but for a long charade. I was going through the motions of an important enterprise: I was acting as if the coming-to-be of the new Church was a matter of significance: I was discussing and making my plans with a good deal of care. But less and less could I put my heart into it: and the intensity of my activity was no more than a compensation for the acuteness of my despair. What was worse, I realised with my head that the feelings of my heart were entirely justified; and that, if they should change, they would do so only at the expense of illusion. I could not hope that I would come to see things in a different light; for I reasoned that I was seeing them now with cool objectivity, and that, if I came to see them differently, I should be seeing them falsely. My subjective depression reflected a calm and objective despair.

My depression reached its lowest depths on a particular evening in the month of May. I was returning from a visit as fruitless and dispiriting as all that had preceded it; and was walking down a road which is still the most pleasant in the district. It was a beautiful evening of early summer, and round me lay the usual scene of innocent contentment. The gardens in which men were working were already showing the promise of high summer, and the children playing on the grass were ruddy with the sun and looked full of health. In front of me was a row of trim new shops; beyond it a wide view of the hills; on my right two schools in spacious and well-kept grounds. Every prospect was of a good world, in which everything was present that was necessary to the happiness and fulfilment of man. But I myself, in my future role, was unnecessary: the cause which I represented was entirely superfluous. It was probably because I felt my irrelevance that I suddenly crossed the road – to the side on which the schools bordered and on which there were, at the moment, no people. I remember the exact spot at which I crossed.

As I did so, I experienced, in one moment, a sudden and complete revolution of attitude. It was as if my world turned upside down: or as if, having long been perplexed by

looking at a picture upside down, I suddenly saw it the
right way up, and understood it. What I saw was still the
same – a good world, full of innocent contentment and
human fulfilment: but I suddenly realised that its goodness
made the presence of the Church not less important but
much more so, not empty of significance but more than ever
full. It was still clear to me that people did not want the
Church or need it: but now it was equally clear that it was
most important that the Church should come to be in the
new district, and should continue in being. The clarity with
which I saw this was an intellectual clarity: I knew that I
was not simply experiencing a change of feeling, but was
seeing something that justified a change of feeling.
Something had been shown to me which I could not but
trust. It was beyond me at the moment to say what this
was: it was simply something which, while affirming the
already-present happiness and fulfilment of the district,
also affirmed the importance of the coming-to-be and of the
presence of the Church. This I could not but trust: for I was
aware not only that my feelings had radically changed but
also, and with equal force, that this change was wholly
justified. I had discovered – or, rather, I had been shown –
that the importance of the Church lies in something other
than its service to, or satisfaction of, the needs of man.

For the time being this conviction emerged in action
rather than reflection: or, more exactly, it invested action
with an entirely new sense of purpose. From that moment I
could do with steady enthusiasm what before had been
done of mere necessity; and this enthusiasm led me to do
what my conviction demanded rather than to reflect upon
what it meant. A period began of intense activity, during
which the Church came into being and engaged the interest, the support and eventually the devotion of a good
many people: a period in which my own time and energies
were entirely absorbed in practical matters. Months passed

into years before I could begin to reflect upon that which had been shown, and to ask myself why, and in what sense, the Church was important. It was no longer important in the senses in which, in my previous experience, it had been important. Yet that it was important was a conviction which I could not but trust. I knew that sometime I must unravel that conviction and try to understand it.

2. The Identification of the Problem

There is a conventional Christian doctrine that the Church lives, or ought to live, 'to the glory of God'. It is not easy to determine with precision what the phrase 'to the glory of God' means: but the doctrine is often used to repudiate, or at least to supplement, the notion that the Church exists simply for the benefit of its members and the service of the world beyond. When members of the Church complain that certain aspects of its worship are unhelpful to them and certain aspects of its life of no social value, they are often reminded that the Church exists not to please or edify themselves, nor to improve society, but to 'glorify God'.

The conviction which transformed my attitude to my new work seemed, at first, no more than a vivid and timely apprehension of this familiar doctrine: and I could find no better words in which to express it. For the moment I was content to say that the purpose of the Church was to serve the glory of God, and to find myself in apparent agreement with many who had reflected on the meaning and the mission of the Church. So long as practical activity took precedence over reflection, the phrase 'to the glory of God' served well enough as a slogan in which to express the purpose of my own work and the goal for the aspiration of the new Church.

But in the course of time the nature of this practical activity began to expose the inadequacy of the slogan to explain or justify it. For, in the first place, this activity was often exercised over matters of minute detail. In the early days of a Church, or of any other institution, the absence of precedents and the lack of tradition brings it about that everything is a matter for decision; and countless hours are spent in discussing and arranging details of order, procedure and equipment. To evade this task is to invite confusion and regret in the future. My fellow-workers in the new Church showed no inclination to evade it: they seemed to share my own sense of the importance of the Church, and were eager to spend time and energy in attending to matters of detail. They were eager to make, for the ordering of worship and the conduct of Church affairs, the best provision of which they were capable: and in this sense they might be said to be offering their energies and resources 'to the glory of God'. But sometimes, at the end of a long and thoughtful discussion, I was compelled to ask myself what, in fact, had been achieved. The outcome of so much thought would not be the emergence of some great work of art or the offering of worship of sublime and unearthly beauty; it would be the provision of a fresh coat of paint on the brick wall behind the altar, or of a decent carpet to deaden the sound of feet. While I could believe that God is glorified in some sublime expression of human creativity, I found it less easy to believe that He is glorified in a freshly painted wall. It was at this humble and even trivial level of creativity that the new Church lived: the best that it could give was of the most prosaic and ordinary kind. The intention was good and worthy: but the subject of our discussion was not intention but execution – whether one colour of paint would be more seemly than another: and this we decided by the imperfect criterion of our own taste. The best that we would achieve by our discussions and labours was modest improvement in the style and appearance of a common-place building and of the activity which went on within it. It seemed to me more and more incongruous to relate, in any way, such trifling achievement to the glory of God.

In the second place, as I came to know my colleagues and fellow-workers, I came to realise that their activity as members of the Church was different only in detail from the activities in which they had previously been engaged. The typical family which came to worship in the Church was a family which, on previous Sundays, had walked, in equal harmony and mutual affection, along the nearby lanes. The typical chorister in the Church was a person already interested in music; and the typical person who undertook the care of the Church building and its garden was a person already useful in the community and in the service of his neighbours. The place of activity was different: its quality was much the same. Activity took a different form: the spirit which animated it seemed little different. This impression of my fellow-workers confirmed what I had already come to expect. I had concluded months before that the district was a place of happy and contented people, living together in neighbourly good-will, conscious of the responsibilities as well as the privilege of belonging to a community. It is true that, as time went by, I came to see that in this community, as in others, there were elements of conflict, deprivation and discontent. But these elements appeared hardly at all in those people who gathered around, and formed, the Church. The activity of the Church itself was the activity of people who, on the whole, were already leading full, useful and satisfying lives.

On one occasion I read an account of the early years of a Methodist Church which was founded in the same town some eighty years before. The motive of its founder was the 'ungodly wretchedness' which he saw daily in walking through a particular quarter of the town. He was moved to thought and action. He began to speak at the doors of pubs and doss-houses and to invite all who heard to break with their past and to begin a new life in and through the simple Meeting House which he had secured. His efforts met with abuse, but also with a measure of success: and the book which I read recorded with honest and just pride the material and moral transformation which, in the ensuing months and years, was evident in many lives. It seemed to me that this kind of radical transformation might well 'glorify God'. For the elimination of the material and moral squalor of a number of human lives would be a significant furtherance of the purpose of a God of love and justice, and a significant contribution and service to His glory. But this was very different from what was happening in my own situation. In the one case there was a profound change in the motives, quality and direction of a number of lives: in the other no more than a modest rearrangement of the details. Again it appeared incongruous to relate, in any way, such trifling rearrangement to the glory of God.

I was convinced that to do so would be to degrade and trivialise the concept of God. If one were realistic about the actual activity and actual achievement of the Church, one could think of it as glorifying God only at the expense of thinking meanly and trivially of God. It seemed that our small, parochial activities could only 'glorify' a God Who was 'peculiarly interested' in the Church: Who had, as it were, a sectarian preference for this particular enclave within the whole of reality: Who, having ordained the Church for His own satisfaction, found a special significance in the activity of man as soon as it was formally incorporated within that which He had ordained. If the Church as I knew it in practice was glorifying God, then the God who was thereby glorified seemed all too like the aging actor who is gratified by the recognition and applause of however small an audience, or the monarch who watches with peculiar interest and concern the manoeuvres of his Household Cavalry. Such offensive analogies came all too readily to mind when I began to reflect upon my own slogan that the modest activities of the Church, and the trifling difference which they made to the life of the district, were a service to, or enhancement of, 'the glory of God'.

The problem was one of disproportion. My view of the Church was necessarily realistic and free of the romanticism which would be possible in a different situation. I was not concerned with the significance of the historic Church of God, rich in tradition and achievement. I was concerned with one new fragment of it, which had come into being so recently that I could see precisely what difference it had made, and was making, to the life of the district. I was still gripped by the conviction that this difference was of great significance, of great importance: but I could not interpret or understand this importance. The presence of the Church could be of no great social or psychological importance; for already, in its absence, the neighbourhood had shown all the marks of a happy and contented community. I concluded, therefore, that the Church must be of an importance which in some sense transcended its limited social and psychological importance: it must be important to something other than the general well-being of its members and of the community at large. But if I identified this 'something other' with God, I was at once aware of a disparity or disproportion or incongruity. It was hard to take seriously the proposition that the colour we chose to apply to a brick wall was of importance to Him Who is the source and ground of all being, the Eternal, the Almighty, the Unconditional.

Yet if the Church were not important to the well-being of man, and if it could not be important to the being of God, to what, and in what sense, could it be important? To this dilemma one very simple answer presented itself, at least as a possibility. The Church, though unimportant to man's temporal well-being, might be important to his eternal salvation. It might be the Ark in which a few, the faithful, are carried through death into the life of the world to come.

It might make little difference to a man's life on earth, but a profound and decisive difference to his eternal destiny.

In any situation there would be difficulties in accepting this interpretation of the mission and purpose of the Church: but in the situation in which I was placed the difficulties were insurmountable. For I was acutely aware, in the first place, that life in the Church was different only in detail from life outside it: and, in the second place, that the presence of some people within the Church, and the absence of others, owed much to factors of chance and circumstance. This second point weighed particularly heavily. In many cases I knew the occasion of a person's first association with the Church: and I knew how often chance rather than choice had determined this occasion. It was repugnant to belief in a God of love and justice that chance-passengers in the Ark should be so richly rewarded, and those who, equally by chance, were absent so heavily penalised. If the new Church were God's instrument for selecting, identifying or preserving those who should be saved, then it was a crude and random instrument. To assert that God so intended or so used the Church would be to degrade and brutalise the concept of God.

I pursued no further this kind of answer to my dilemma. I began to suspect that, if a satisfactory answer were to be found, it would be found within that very situation in which the dilemma itself had arisen. The dilemma – or at least one half of it – had arisen out of the fact that the difference which the Church made to the life of the district was so small a difference; that the life of the Church itself was so little different from the general life and activity of the community. There was a *continuity* between the Church and the world outside the Church: both were made of the same stuff – of things and people and the actions of people: the Church was of a piece with its environment. Whatever else the Church might be, it was certainly a part of material reality: it was an arrangement of people and things – all of which might have been arranged in a different way. Therefore the Church must be at least as important as the things out of which it was made. This truth could be expressed in religious terms by saying that, whatever else the Church was, it was certainly a part of the creation; and therefore that it must share whatever importance might belong to created things in general.

During the nineteen sixties the importance of created things in general was beginning to exercise the practical concern of many people. The duty of 'the conservation of nature' was beginning to be proclaimed by many voices. In general, this duty was not represented as a religious duty, and those who proclaimed it made no use of explicitly religious terms or categories. Very often the duty was presented as simply a rule of prudence: a care for nature was represented as important to the present and future well-being of mankind. Scientists and naturalists were able to show that the exploitation and abuse of the natural world might have consequences more serious, and sometimes more immediate, than had previously been suspected: and that, even where no specific harm could be detected to the well-being of mankind, there might be disturbance to the 'balance of nature' – of which the consequences, being unforeseeable, might be extremely serious. It became a commonplace that the order of nature is a finely-balanced system; and that the maintenance of this balance is of great importance to the well-being, and even to the survival, of mankind. Therefore prudence dictated not merely the avoidance of those particular abuses of nature of which the consequences could be foreseen; but also a general respect and care for the world of nature as a whole and for every particular aspect of it. Although the preservation of a species or a habitat might seem at present to bring no benefit to mankind, it might prove in the long run of the greatest importance to human survival and welfare.

But sometimes particular enterprises of conservation seemed to be motivated by something other than a prudent concern for the long-term welfare of mankind. Naturalists sometimes acted as if the preservation of a species or habitat were 'an end in itself'. In advocating its preservation, they did not attempt to show its decisive place within the chain and balance of nature: they simply demonstrated how near it was to extinction. They argued as if its survival were important in itself, irrespective of any benefit that might accrue to human well-being. Some advocated the preservation of 'wilderness' – that is to say, of areas of the earth from which human beings would be virtually excluded: others worked for the survival of species which could survive only in isolation from mankind. In order that a species might survive, some naturalists devoted endless labour to the study of its habits: and could only 'justify' their labours by the circular argument that, if the species survived, it would still be there for future naturalists to study. Whatever the formal arguments might be of workers in the cause of conservation, it was hard to avoid the conclusion that, in certain cases, they were motivated by the sense of a worth or importance in natural objects which could not, in the last analysis, be reduced to their worth or importance to man.

It might be argued that, when a naturalist asserts that a rare species is important, or that its survival is important, he is simply asserting his own interest in it: that he is saying no more than that the species interests him and that its survival is important to his own intellectual or aesthetic satisfaction. But often a naturalist will offer what appear to be objective grounds for the importance of the species in question – that, for instance, it is unique in its breeding habits: that it is unusual in anatomical structure: that it is the beginning or the end of a certain line of evolutionary development. Thus he argues as if the importance of the species is in some sense 'built into' it, and is the cause rather than the consequence of his own interest and enthusiasm. Furthermore, the zeal of conservationists for the education of the public presupposes that the more people know about the things of nature the more they will respect them; and this in turn implies that, in coming to know the details of what a species or a creature is, people will also come to know that it deserves respect, or that it is important. One detects within the conservationist movement the hidden premise that the detail of nature contains the clue to the importance of nature: so that to know the first is to become aware of the second. Whereas the romantic movement asserted the importance of nature through the idealisation of nature, the movement of conservation discovers the importance of nature through the minute and realistic examination of its detail.

Increasingly, over a number of years, I came to feel a certain similarity between my own activity and that of some naturalists and practical conservationists. When I met such a person, or heard on the radio a description of his work, I sensed immediately a 'kindred spirit'. Each of us was absorbed in *tending* a fragment within the totality of material being. I was tending a Church: the naturalist was tending a patch of marsh or woodland, or a few remaining members of a declining species. Each of us felt the importance of that fragment with which he was concerned: but neither of us could explain that importance in terms of importance to the well-being of mankind. Each of us felt a responsibility which could not be reduced, directly or indirectly, to responsibility to or for our fellow men. And for each of us our work involved a minute and realistic attention to the finest detail of that with which we were engaged. Whether or not we were alike in our psychological motivation, we were alike, it seemed, in the internal logic of our activity.

Therefore, I came to believe that I could understand the importance of my own 'fragment' only if I could also understand the importance of the kind of fragment with which a naturalist might be concerned. On one occasion I heard a talk by a naturalist about his minute and patient observation of a dying tree: and so a dying tree in my own district, which I frequently passed, became for me the symbol or representative of that with which the naturalist is concerned. It was one of the few trees which survived from before the time when the new houses were built: its roots had probably been disturbed in the course of building: its trunk had been hacked by children: the hollow in which it stood served as a rubbish dump: many of its branches had already died and fallen. It was no longer beautiful: soon it would die altogether, rot and eventually fall. Many times, as I passed this tree, I asked myself about its importance, its meaning, its significance.

I knew of the God without Whom no sparrow falls to the ground. I could conceive, as a logical or theological possibility, that my tree, like the sparrow, might be important to God. But always the problem arose of disproportion or incongruity. It was very difficult to hold together, on the one hand, a vision of God which was not a trivialisation of God; and, on the other hand, the meagre and stunted leaves of this particular tree. It was one thing to believe that God created all things, but another to believe that this 'fag-end' of His creation could be important to Him. When man creates a road, he glories in its sweep and scale; but he has no concern for a particular pebble on its surface. Always the problem of disproportion remained.

I have noticed over many years that the progress of quite serious thinking may be assisted by incidents of the most ordinary and even trivial kind. So it was in the present case. On a winter morning two schoolboys in their early teens asked me to suggest an occupation for their half-term holiday. I was unprepared and rather barren of ideas; but eventually, having once occupied myself in the same way, I suggested that they might make a model of a tract of countryside. I reminded them of an area around a waterfall in the West of Ireland which both they and I had recently visited: I explained how a model might be made out of stones and twigs and plaster and paint: I offered them a room in which to work, and I told them where they might find the necessary materials.

My suggestion made no great appeal, and it was taken up out of courtesy rather than enthusiasm. Enthusiam was even less when the two had assembled their rather unattractive raw materials of stones from the street, dead twigs and old paint in dirty cans. Nevertheless, they began to work that same morning; returned in the afternoon and again in the evening; and by the end of the day they had something which they wanted to show me. Something was beginning to take shape. Next morning they came early; and thereafter, for three days, they worked with remarkable intensity and concentration, without thought of mealtimes or the lateness of the hour. From time to time I watched and listened. I observed how the placing of each stone and twig was a matter for careful discussion. Each was, as it were, surveyed and its possibilities assessed. One would be split or cut so that it would fit a certain place. It would be placed: and then came the moment of waiting to see if it was 'right'. It would be agreed that a certain stone should be painted to give the appearance of moss: and it would be agreed that a certain mixture of paint was right. But still one had to wait and see whether the stone would take the paint without distorting its colour; and again whether, when placed, the painted stone 'looked right'. Some stones and twigs and details of plaster-work proved 'difficult': they had possibilities but would not easily 'come right'. Again, a stone might appear 'right' until another was placed beside it: but then a difficulty appeared, and with it a new possibility: and the first stone must be repainted or replaced. The detail of the once unattractive and even contemptible material now became important: the dirt on a twig could prove 'just right' for shadow on the branch of a tree: spilled plaster could be made into rocks at the foot of the waterfall. In everything there was the possibility both of 'difficulty' and of 'coming right': and the full possibility of each fragment must be discovered and tried in relation to other fragments.

As the model grew and became of greater value, each step in its creation became of greater moment and was taken with greater intensity of care. Each item that was placed seemed to possess greater power to make or to mar. The two workers came to have, as it were, less room for manoeuvre: they worked less but watched and waited more. Having expended to the full their own power to make, they became the more attentive to what the model itself might disclose. They came to discover that which they were making, and to be affected by that which they discovered. The once contemptible sticks and stones now had a certain power over those who were using them – a power to effect or negate the completion of that which was being made, and so to satisfy or frustrate those who were making it. The two boys became vulnerable in and through that which, out of virtually nothing, they had brought into being. They became concerned for the safety of their model, anxious lest anyone coming into the room might touch and spoil it. They would permit the privilege of seeing it only to certain people who would have the discernment and sensitivity to appreciate it. When eventually the model was left in my care, I felt a quite serious responsibility for its safety.

As I watched this microcosm of creative activity, and as later I reflected upon it, three things gradually became evident to me. The first was that, in such activity, there was both working and waiting. One could say that the activity of creating included the passivity of waiting – of waiting upon one's workmanship to see what emerged from it, and to see if that which emerged was 'right'. The second, which followed from the first, was that, in such activity, the creator gave to, or built into, his workmanship a certain power over himself. He gave to his workmanship that which, if it were not his workmanship, it would not possess– a power to affect himself, to have value, significance or importance for himself. The third, which followed from the second, was that in such activity disproportion between creator and workmanship, or between creator and material, was overcome by the gift of value. That which in itself was nothing was transformed, in the creative process, into a thing of value: as the work of a creator, it received a new status in relation to the creator. The incongruity between the great and the small was overcome when the creativity of the great was expended in and upon the small.

The activity which I had watched involved no great skill, and its outcome was of no *aesthetic* value. It was not because skill had worked upon the sticks and stones, and beauty emerged from them, that they had become 'greater' in relation to the two human beings who had been engaged upon them. What had impressed me as observer was not the imaginative talent of the two workers, or the skill of their hands: it was the total concentration upon their work of such talent as they possessed, their obliviousness of mealtimes and of their own tiredness, their expenditure upon the one task of the whole of their energy and care. One might say that, for the creation of the model, the two had given themselves. If, through skill or practice, they had made the same model more easily, it would have lacked the particular value which it now possessed: there would not have been 'built into' it the self-giving of its creators. The same model, mass produced in a factory or casually constructed in the idle moments of a skilled workman, would have been of no importance; and for its safety I should have felt no sense of responsibility.

For the self-giving built into the model I could find no simple word or name but love. It was love which had overcome the disproportion between the creators and their workmanship, between human beings and sticks from the dustbin or stones from the gutter. It was love which had given importance to the sticks and stones, and, to myself, a sense of responsibility for them. I, the observer, perceived the importance of the model, and my own responsibility for it, because I knew it to be the work of love. I had actually seen the activity of love – the concentration, the effort and the unsparingness of self-giving that are involved in love. If I had simply been told that the model was the work of love, and if I had know little of what love involves, then my sense of the importance of the model, and of my own responsibility for it, would have been less strong. It was because I had seen what love involves that I knew that the model was no trivial thing.

Therefore, through this simple incident, I was helped to see that awareness of the importance of any aspect of material reality may be awareness not of its relevance to human well-being but simply of its being the work of love: and that a sense of responsibility for it may be a sense of responsibility for a work of love. My own awareness of the importance of that fragment of material reality which is the Church, and the naturalist's awareness of the importance of that fragment of material reality which is a particular marsh or pond or wood, might be awareness, however indistinct, of the whole of material reality as the work of love. I asked myself why I had needed several years and the adventitious help of a boys' holiday task to reach this simple and prosaic conclusion. I was compelled to answer that not until now had I realised what creative love is like. I had been told that material reality is the workmanship of the love of God: but when that love had been described to me it was different from that which I had seen built into the schoolboys' model. That which had been described to me as the love of God did not justify or explain the importance of that which it was alleged to have created. Therefore I knew that I must seek for a better description of the love of God – a description that might explain that conviction which, though unexplained and not yet unravelled, was still with me and still beyond doubt or question – the conviction of the importance of that small and simple fragment of material reality which is the Church.

If I could find such a description, it would make plain the importance not of the Church in particular but of material reality in general. Whether it would also point to some peculiar and distinctive importance in the Church was another matter. If it did not, my enquiry would prove in vain – or, at best, incomplete. But I knew the Church best in its concrete and material being – as a building to be cared for, as people in one place rather than another, as certain words said and certain actions performed: and it was of this concrete and material fragment that I was attempting to discover the importance. I thought it unlikely that I should do so unless I could first discover the generic importance of material reality: only by this way, it seemed, would it be possible to discover the specific importance of the Church.

3. The Phenomenology of Love

It is a commonplace of Christian preaching that 'the love of God is broader than the measure of man's mind'. Few preachers would use an instance or expression of love between human beings as an adequate and perfect illustration of the love of God. Most preachers would say that the love of God 'surpasses' or 'transcends' human love: some would say that it is 'altogether different from' human love.

This last statement cannot be taken seriously. If the love of God is altogether different from human love, then it would be better to use for it the name of something from which it is not altogether different – the name of something within our experience to which it bears some likeness: and if there is nothing within our experience to which it bears some likeness, then were are speaking of a wholly unknown 'something' of which it is unprofitable to speak.

The reason, though not the justification, for the use of such exaggerated and even meaningless language is, of course, simple. We are well aware that, in the relationship between man and man, many things masquerade as love: and that that which is offered or described as love often fails to 'ring true'. It would indeed be foolish to use in illustration of the love of God each and every human activity or attitude which claims the name of love: for there is no name which is so unjustly usurped or so often misused.

Our human awareness of the misuse of the word 'love' and of its usurpation by that which is not authentic love is remarkable. A deprived child, who apparently has never known the authenticity of love, will yet recognise its falsity. With love it is not as with food – that those who are hungry will be satisfied with anything. On the contrary, those who are deprived of love are the most demanding and dis- criminating in what they will receive. A child hungry for love is most quick to detect and reject condescension, bribery or manipulation when it masquerades as love, and requires most full assurance of the authenticity of that which is offered to him. Though he has never tasted authen- tic love, he knows already the taste of what he needs.

Neither emotional deprivation nor simplicity of mind precludes this remarkable power of discrimination. In the matter of love, a simple person is no easier to deceive than a person of intelligence and sophistication. A backward child knows as well as an intelligent adult when he is being used. He will not express in words what he knows; but anyone who has so used such a child has seen the downcast eyes and the hurt face. Simple people will often use the most subtle means to test the authenticity of love: they will feign all kinds of helplessness and distress to test the care of love, and will offer subtle provocation to see if love is hurt. Even the helpless victim of brain damage, otherwise insensitive and without power of discrimination, seems aware of the presence or absence of authentic love. One may suspect that the power to distinguish and recognise love extends beyond mankind into certain of the animal species: certain- ly it seems to be universal among mankind. Since authentic love is so potent a support of life, the power to distinguish it from its destructive imitations has perhaps evolved as a necessity for survival.

It may be noticed in passing that pretences and parodies of love are not only recognised: they are also resented. What a man will accept when it is presented under its true colours will be an affront when it is disguised as love. Most people are willing, and even glad, to be of use to other people; and are ready to make their skill or knowledge available to another who seeks help or counsel. But when the benefit of their skill or knowledge is obtained under the masquerade of love or the guise of friendship there is immediate and just resentment. Most people will accept the overt and direct instruction of a superior: but the instruction of a superior is resented if it purports to be the advice of a friend. The pre-eminent worth of authentic love makes the affectation of love the most damaging and the most resented of all deceptions.

The power to test and recognise the authenticity of love is, in most people, a practical instinct or skill rather than an intellectual capacity. The deprived child cannot describe what he is looking for, although he knows when it is absent. But reflection can detect, within the practical discrimination of mankind, a certain pattern of activity or frame of reference. That love which man seeks can be described, at least by approximation, by detecting a pattern in that which he rejects or which fails to satisfy him. It is as if, by examining the rejects from a certain mechanical operation, one should describe what the machine is designed to make: or as if, by examining a number of broken and variously distorted bones, one should describe a complete and perfect skeleton. It may be, as preachers remind us, that we have never met, in human experience, perfectly authentic love. Nevertheless we may extrapolate, from the distortions which are rejected, the form which authentic love must take. The word 'phenomenological' is peculiarly appropriate to such a description of love: for the word 'phenomenon' is ambiguous. It designates both 'that which is shown' and 'that which appears to be': it points both to authenticity and to mere appearance. When we give an account of the authentic by detecting a pattern in that which is rejected as mere appearance, then our method may properly be described as phenomenological: and it is a method appropriate to the study of love because there exists in man a practical power to detect and reject that which is mere appearance. It is another matter whether the phenomenological method is proper or even possible in other fields of enquiry: but it is a proper method of enquiry into the form and nature of authentic love.

The description in which the enquiry ends cannot be shown to be true: for, at least according to the preachers, there is no criterion, no experience of perfectly authentic love, against which it can be checked. It cannot be shown to be trustworthy: but it will in fact be trusted precisely to the extent that it does justice to the actual operation of the practical power of discrimination: to the extent that it accurately identifies those distortions which are recognised and rejected as such, and provides the most economical pattern into which, if free from distortion, those distorted elements will fit. It will in fact be trusted unless it errs in identifying that which is rejected, or unless the pattern of authenticity which it detects can be expressed in yet more economical form.

If we can describe the form of authentic love, we can hardly look elsewhere for a description of the love of God. If we can say 'what love ought to be', we need enquire no further what the love of God is. Any further question would be profitless and even meaningless enquiry into 'an unknown something'.

When we reflect upon the practical power of discrimination, we discover three marks or signs which are recognised as denying the authenticity of love. The first is the mark of limitation. That which professes to be love is exposed as false if it is recognised as limited. Another name is given to it – the name of 'kindness' or 'benevolence'. 'Kindness' under its own name is usually welcome: but it becomes an affront when it masquerades as love. When love dies kindness often becomes its substitute – a substitute which, being recognised under the disguise of love, is thrown back in the face. When love is expected, no kindness, however lavish, satisfies: for it is known that, however much is given, something is being withheld. A locked room or a locked box will affront someone to whom, in the name of love, all the rest of the house has been made open: a secret of which one will not speak will offend someone to whom, in the guise of love, one will disclose everything else.

When a person, longing to be loved, tests the authenticity of love, he will often erect barriers to see if love will overcome them, or propose limits to see if love will transcend them. Having discovered that love will transcend such and such a barrier or limit, he will erect or propose another. In a neurotic person this quest for assurance becomes an endless obsession: it is necessarily endless for the person is attempting to 'prove a negative' – to establish that there is *no* limit to that which will be given, endured or done. In a deprived child the testing of love often consists of erecting the barrier or limit of outrageous behaviour on his own part – of offending to see if he is still accepted, of running away from home to see if he is sought. In the mythology of love, the hero's love is tested by the prescription of tasks, each more daunting than the last, each serving as a barrier or limit to be transcended in the proving of love. In the teaching of Christ love is shown to express itself in *endless* forgiveness. Whereas a kind man will forgive up to seven times, a loving man will forgive times without number. In many ways and forms, the authenticity of love is tested against the possibility that that which is represented as love is, in fact, limited. No such test can be decisive for the authenticity of love: but any test can be decisive for its falsity.

When we love, we are aware that every word and action on our part, being itself limited, fails to express the fullness of love. In the poetry of love, the typical expression of love is the proposal of some metaphor or analogy of that love –

followed by repudiation of that metaphor or analogy as inadequate. In the making of a gift of love, we are careful to suggest, by the manner in which the gift is given, or by the words which accompany it, that the gift itself, however precious, is no more than a symbol of that which we would express. In the person whom we love, we welcome the new sensitivity, the enlargement of understanding or even of need, which will give opportunity for a new and larger expression of love. Never, when we love, do we welcome the situation which sets *narrower* limits to what love can do and give – the situation in which all that we can do or give is little and costs little. Always the aspiration of love is to enlarge the limits of that field within which, through circumstances, its expression must be restricted.

Among the circumstances which restrict the expression of love is the capacity of the other to receive. A parent knows the danger of overwhelming or imprisoning a child by expressions of love which are untimely or excessive. A friend knows that expressions of friendship too sudden or demonstrative may simply embarrass. A wife knows that, out of love for her husband, she must sometimes 'think about herself'. The external restraint which love practices is often a mark of its freedom from internal limit. Love does not lay down the condition that it must be allowed freedom to express itself, nor limit its activity to those circumstances in which it may freely act. Love accepts without limit the discipline of circumstances. Although it always aspires to enlarge its own activity, it sometimes finds its most generous enlargement in the acceptance of restraint. Love must sometimes express itself in the renunciation of not disclosing itself.

That which love withholds is withheld for the sake of the other who is loved – so that it may not harm him, so that it may be used for a more timely service or so that it may mature into a richer gift. A person who loves holds nothing for himself: he reserves nothing as of right. That which he holds, he holds either on trust or as gift. He holds on trust that which awaits its own maturity or the need or capacity of the other to receive it: he holds as gift that which is returned to him in the response of the other who is loved. The enrichment which many discover in the experience of loving is not an enlargement of rights or an increase in possession: it is the discovery as trust or gift of that which had previously been known only as possession. When a person loves, all that is in his power is invested with a sense of purpose, as available for the other, or becomes a cause or occasion of gratitude, as received by gift from the other.

The falsity of love is exposed wherever any limit is set by the will of him who professes to love: wherever, by his will, something is withheld. Therefore the authenticity of love must imply a totality of giving – that which we call the giving of self or self-giving. The self is the totality of what a man has and is: and it is no less than this that is offered or made available in love. When we become aware that something less than the self is offered, we become aware of the falsity of love.

The second mark which denies the authenticity of love is the mark of control. When one who professes to love is wholly in control of the object of his love, then the falsity of love is exposed. Love is activity for the sake of an *other*: and where the object of love is wholly under the control of the one who loves, that object is no longer an other. It is a part or extension of the professed lover – an extension of himself. A widow professes her love for her only son – now a man of mature years: she explains that she knows him through and through: that he depends upon her in everything and 'cannot manage' without her. She claims that, in his career, she has 'got him where he is': that he is 'quite content as he is', and that, so long as she lives, he will not think of marriage. We may suspect that the widow's assurance is not wholly justified, and that her 'hold' upon her son is more precarious than she claims. But we know that, if her assurance is justified, her love is an extended selfishness. When she thinks of her son, she excludes the possibility of a clash of wills or interests: what is 'his' is a part of what is 'hers' – an inseparable part of an extended self ruled by her will. Love has become distorted by the assurance of possession and control.

Where the object of love is truly an 'other', the activity of love is always precarious. Between the self and the other there always exists, as it were, a 'gap' which the aspiration of love may fail to bridge or transcend. That which love would do or give or express may fail to 'arrive' – through misjudgement, through misunderstanding or through rejection. Love may be 'frustrated': its most earnest aspirations may 'come to nothing': the greatness of what is offered in love may be wholly disproportionate to the smallness of that, if anything, which is received. Herein lies the poignancy of love, and its potential tragedy. The activity of love contains no assurance or certainty of completion: much may be expended and little achieved. The progress of love must always be by tentative and precarious steps: and each step that is taken, whether it 'succeeds' or 'fails', becomes the basis for the next, and equally precarious, step which must follow.

Love proceeds by no assured programme. In the care of children a parent is peculiarly aware that each step of love is a step of risk; and that each step taken generates the need for another and equally precarious step. In each word of encouragement lies the danger of creating over-confidence: in each restraint the danger of destroying confidence. A risk is taken when a child is allowed to ride his bicycle on the road: when he returns in pride and confidence, the gain has justified the risk. But now there is a new danger of over-confidence, and the child must be warned – yet not so severely that his new-found confidence is destroyed. In each expression of love to a child lies the danger that it will be exploited and that the child will be 'spoiled' by taking as a right that which should be received as a gift: in each withholding of love's expression lies the danger of misunderstanding – the danger that that which was meant to teach will serve only to embitter and estrange. A happy family life is neither a static situation nor a smooth and direct progression: it is an angular progress, the endless improvisation of love to correct that which it has itself created. Parents will testify that their equal love for two children must express itself in quite different ways; and that what they have learned in bringing up the elder can be no programme for bringing up the younger. The care of children teaches us that the resolute and unfailing will of love becomes active in improvised and ever-precarious endeavour.

The precariousness of love's activity appears equally clearly in the field of artistic creation. It may be said of the artist that he is always stretching his powers beyond their known limit. If he works within his limit, proceeding by an assured programme and doing only that which he knows himself able to do, then he is no longer a creative artist: and his work falls into the category of reproduction or manufacture. In his activity the artist discovers his own capacity: but his capacity is not to be thought of as a fixed quantity, nor his activity as an experiment to detect the limit of that quantity. His work is not experiment but engagement – engagement which enlarges that which it employs by the risk of extending it beyond its known capacity. As the artist exceeds his known powers, his work is precariously poised between success and failure, between triumph and tragedy: it may be that the work of art is marred beyond redemption, or it may be that powers hitherto unknown will prove adequate to the completion and triumph of the work. As we watch a painter at work, or as we follow the unfolding of a poet's theme, there comes the moment of the bold brushstroke or the adventurous image: and at that moment the work as a whole is thrown out of balance. The brushstroke seems excessively heavy, the image merely bizarre. If creative activity should be interrupted at that point, we should see the whole work marred, and the artist fall victim to his excess of boldness. But often it is precisely at that moment that we see the greatness of the artist: we see him able to triumph through his apparent excess – to use the brushstroke as the beginning of a new area of depth or radiance within the picture, to develop the image so that it becomes integral to an enlarged vision. We suspect that it was not the intention of the artist so to use and develop what appeared in the moment of excess: that its appearance was to him, as to us, an unexpected and even daunting challenge: that, in the moment when he exceeded his tried and known powers, his work was, in the strictest sense, 'out of control'. But we see the greatness of the artist precisely in his power to win back control, to use that which had gone astray as an element within a new and larger whole. We see, at the moment of lost control, the most intense endeavour of the artist: and his greatness lies in his ability to discover ever-new reserves of power to meet each challenge of precarious adventure – each challenge of powers exceeded and of control lost. As we follow, in actuality or in retrospect, the fashioning of a work of art, we are always conscious of it as poised upon the brink of failure: and if we analyse, into steps or moments, the progress of its creation, we discern that same angular progress as in the care and upbringing of a family. Each decisive step is a precarious step, to be redeemed from tragedy only by the next and equally precarious step, of correction or new discovery, which must be improvised to succeed it.

In artistic creation, as in human relationships, the authenticity of love is denied by the assurance of control. Love aspires to reach that which, being truly an 'other', cannot be controlled. The aspiration of love is that the other, which cannot be controlled, may receive: and the greatness of love lies in its endless and unfailing improvisation in hope that the other may receive. As aspiration, love never fails: for there is no internal limit to its will to endeavour, to venture and to expend. But as specific achievement, love must often fail: and each step it takes is poignant for the possibility of failure. A love which so controlled the other that it could not fail, or which limited its activity to those projects in which it could not fail, would be bereft of all poignancy, and would be exposed as falsity. Where the power to control appears in the guise or masquerade of love, we give to it, depending on the circumstances, such varied names as extended selfishness, manipulation, condescension or, at the very best, courtesy.

The precariousness of love is experienced, subjectively, in the tense passivity of 'waiting'. For the completion of its endeavour, for its outcome as triumph or as tragedy, love must wait. We have already noticed the element of waiting which is present in all artistic creativity: and, in human relationships, it is no accident that, in the most commonplace and popular representations of love, the lover appears as a *waiting* figure. One might even say that the subjective awareness of love appears first as awareness of the necessity of waiting. It is important to see that that for which the lover or the artist waits is not some gain or goal which might have been attained by different means, or some 'reward' for his devoted activity. The 'reward' for which he waits is nothing else than the completion of his own activity – the response of receiving which is the completion of his own activity of giving. For this the lover or the artist must wait: and the necessity of waiting brings home to him the precariousness of his love's endeavour – its lack of final control over that situation which it has itself created. Where control is complete, and exercised in complete assurance, the falsity of love is exposed.

The third mark which denies the authenticity of love is the mark of detachment – of self-sufficiency unaffected and unimpaired in the one who professes to love. Love is *self*-giving: and the self includes power of feeling as well as power of possession and action. Where love withholds from the other power over the feeling self, there the falsity of love is exposed.

Authentic love may *affect* a certain detachment. A sensitive person is aware of the danger of coming to control, possess or dominate an other through the 'blackmail' of his own sensitivity; and of the opposite danger of 'spoiling' an other through the too open exposure of his own sensitivity. Unless a parent affects a certain degree of detachment, a child may be either appalled or tempted by the power to delight or to distress which is given to him. He may be driven to dissimulation in order to discharge the heavy responsibilities which his power brings or to exploit the golden opportunities which it presents. Therefore a parent may best express love by feigning a certain aloofness and indifference, both to the child's tantrums and to his charms. But to the child most hungry for love, this affectation of detachment is intolerable, and he will go to extreme lengths to overcome it. For he will read the detachment as a sign that the love professed for him is false. Either, therefore, he must accept the falsity of love; or, by breaking down the affectation, he must reassure himself of his power to hurt or please, and therefore of the authenticity of the love which is professed. For this reason, those who work among deprived children often discover that their greatest failure is their greatest success: that it is only when patience fails and gives way to anger that a child is reassured: that it is only when they can no longer control their own feelings that the desolate feelings of a child are assuaged. For an adult presiding over a group of deprived children, it is a remarkable experience to observe the healing effect upon the group of his own outburst of anger, self-pity or resentment – an outburst of which he himself may be deeply ashamed.

Where love is authentic, the lover gives to the object of his love a certain power over himself – a power which would not otherwise be there. This truth is neatly illustrated in a homely incident recalled by a woman who, for many years, was 'Auntie', or foster-mother, to a family of children deprived of the care of their natural parents. 'It was when N. was about twelve years old that I heard one evening that he had been stealing. Long before he came home I had heard the whole story and was satisfied that what I had heard was true: so when he came I was waiting at the door for him. I took him by the scruff of the neck, and I threw him into the garden, saying, 'We will have no thieves in this house'. I left him in the garden a long time; and then, when I opened the door and he came in for bed, I kicked him up the stairs. In the morning N. was very chastened and very quiet: but at last he came to me and asked shyly, 'Auntie, after what happened last night, do you still love me?' So of course I said to him, 'Do I still love you? But, N., *of course* I love you. If I did not love you, do you think that you would have made me so angry?'

The boy's power to make 'Auntie' angry was the mark or proof of her love for him. It was also the gift of her love. The boy's power was rooted not in some quality or capacity of his own, but simply in the fact that he was loved. To that which is loved power is given which it would not otherwise possess and which otherwise would be unaccountable. So, in the literature of love, a person of no account in the world's eyes comes to exercise power through being loved by a person great in the world's eyes. This power, of course, is limited in its scope: it is exercised only upon the lover or through the lover, and when the lover dies or his love fades so also dies or fades the power of the beloved.

The power over itself which love gives to its object may be described in various ways. It is power to make angry or to make glad; to cause grief or joy; to frustrate or to fulfill; to determine tragedy or truimph. It is 'power of meaning' – the power of having meaning to, or value for, the one who loves. It is the power of affecting the one who loves. It creates a new vulnerability in the one who loves. This vulnerability exists, of course, only in relationship to the beloved: but it extends throughout the whole range of the lover's capacity to feel and to be affected. Love is less than authentic if any aspect of the lover's sensibility remains invulnerable in and through the beloved.

Not the lover only but love itself is vulnerable in and through the beloved. It is not vulnerable in the sense that it can be diminished or destroyed: for the power to affect is love's own gift, and the power exists only to the extent that love is undiminished. Our love is not diminished by the anger which another causes in us: for that anger lives only because we love: it is the other side of the coin of love. But love is vulnerable in and through the beloved in the sense that in him its issue is at stake – its completion or frustration, its triumph or tragedy. He who loves surrenders into other hands the issue and outcome of his own aspiration – its dénouement as triumph or as tragedy.

Where there is no such surrender or gift of power the falsity of love is exposed. The human power of discrimination is constantly exercised to discern this mark of falsity. The commonplace question, 'Do I matter?' is the question of whether I have power to affect the person who professes to love me or to whose love I feel myself entitled: and a huge range of human behaviour may be interpreted as a variety of attempts to answer the question. Our doubt about the authenticity of love is most commonly raised by, and focussed upon, the apparent detachment of one whose love is sought or expected: and our testing of love is most commonly a testing of the reality of this detachment. As we have seen, some appearance of detachment is often a necessity for the freedom and well-being of the person loved: and therefore such an appearance is very often presented. So it is upon this apparent detachment that our power of discrimination is, in ordinary life, most commonly exercised. Of the three marks of love's falsity which we have detected, it is this third which is most commonly feared, looked for and found – the mark of detachment, or one's own inability to affect the one whose love is sought, of one's inability to 'mean anything' to him or her. Our scrutiny of love professed for us, or sought by us, is, most commonly, the scrutiny of our own 'power of meaning'.

We have detected three marks by which the falsity of love is exposed – the mark of limitation, the mark of control and the mark of detachment. From these we may approximate to a description of authentic love as limitless, as precarious and as vulnerable. None of these three epithets is precise or wholly free from ambiguity: and we should be glad to find words more simple and exact. But perhaps this is not possible. For our description of authentic love is not a description of something which is commonly, or even occasionally, seen, felt or experienced: it is extrapolation or approximation from the shape or pattern of our practical power of discrimination. Seeing that which is rejected in the human search for love, we can approximate towards that which is sought – towards that which love 'ought to be'. It is perhaps proper that our approximation should contain a degree of mistiness and imprecision: for we are describing not that which any man has known or experienced but that towards which every man, at the depth of his being which is more profound than language, gropes and aspires.

4. The Kenosis of God

Three famous lines of the *Dies Irae* contain at the end of each three words which express the limitlessness, the vulnerability and the precariousness of authentic love:-

> Quaerens me sedisti lassus:
> Redemisti, crucem passus:
> Tantus labor non sit cassus.[1]

The word 'lassus' – 'weary' or 'spent' – expresses the limitlessness of love's self-giving: the word 'passus' – 'suffering' – expresses the vulnerability of love: the word 'cassus' – 'in vain' – expresses the precariousness of love and the possibility that its outcome is tragedy and its work in vain.

In the poem the words are addressed to the Redeemer of mankind: and the 'so great labour' to which they refer is the redemption of mankind in general and of the writer in particular. They represent that labour as, in the strictest sense, 'a labour of love'. They express the profound awareness of a Christian man that his own redemption has been achieved at the cost of a 'labour' in which are disclosed the limitlessness, the vulnerability and the precariousness of authentic love. They echo the common awareness of Christendom that the work of the Redeemer is nothing less than the work of authentic and perfect love.

Reflection has interpreted the Redeemer as the Word of

1. 'Spent dids't Thou fall that Thou mightest my soul gain; To save me Thous dids't bear the cross's pain; May not so great a labour be in vain.'

God – as the expression or manifestation of what God is. In a moment of time the Redeemer has disclosed not one aspect of the divine being, nor one moment of the divine history, but the fullness of what God is. The work of redemption may be described as an event in time: but that which is disclosed through it is not 'divine event' (if such a phrase may be allowed to have any meaning) but divine being. Whatever characterises the event or work of redemption characterises also, through and through, the being and activity of God.

Scripture speaks of the Redeemer as 'emptying Himself': and Christology has ventured to interpret the coming of the Redeemer as a divine 'self-emptying', or Kenosis. Strong objection has been raised to this interpretation – objection which seems to be based on the proposition that the fullness of God cannot be revealed in One Who, having 'emptied Himself', is less than God. But such objection is overcome if the God Who is revealed is the very God who 'empties Himself' – Whose whole and total activity is the activity of self-emptying, or Kenosis. The Kenosis of the Redeemer, His surrender of that which He might have held, will then be the perfect manifestation of the Kenosis of God. The 'emptiness' of the Redeemer, in the poverty and humility of His historical existence, will point to the 'emptiness' of God in and through His eternal activity: and the Kenosis in Christ, so far from impairing the fullness of His disclosure of God, will in fact contain the very heart and substance of that disclosure.

The purpose of this chapter is to reflect upon the love of God in the light of that description of authentic love which was achieved in the last chapter. We have observed that, when Christian devotion contemplates the Redeemer, it attributes to His 'labour' a limitlessness, a vulnerability and a precariousness which mark it as the labour of authentic love. We have also observed that, when Christian theology interprets the person of the Redeemer, it sees in Him a full and perfect disclosure of the nature and activity of God. Therefore Christianity should have no hesitation in attributing to God that authenticity of love which it recognises in His Christ – in attributing to the Creator that authenticity of love which it recognises in the Redeemer. In other words, the phrase 'the love of God' should be associated, in full seriousness and in full understanding of its meaning, not only with the 'labour' of redemption but with the totality of that divine activity which is the ground and source and origin of all that is. We may emphasise this association by suggesting that the Kenosis of the Redeemer points to, and is the manifestation of, the Kenosis of the Creator: and we may describe as 'The Kenosis of God' that activity of authentic love which is the activity of God in creation.

The activity of God in creation must be limitless creativity. It must set no interior limit to its own self-giving. It must ever seek to enlarge the capacity to receive of that 'other' to which it gives. The infinity of the universe must be understood, with awe, as the expression or the consequence of the limitlessness of the divine self-giving: for the divine aspiration to give must ever enlarge the bounds of that which is to receive. Nothing must be withheld from the self-giving which is creation: no unexpended reserves of divine power or potentiality: no 'glory of God' or 'majesty of God' which may be compared and contrasted with the glory of the galaxies and the majesty of the universe: no 'power of God' which might exceed and over-ride the God-given powers of the universe: no 'eternity of God' which might outlive an eternal universe. It is to be understood that the universe is not to be equated with 'that which science knows', nor even with 'that which science might, in principle, come to know': the universe is the totality of being for which God gives Himself in love. From

His self-giving nothing is held back: nothing remains in God unexpended.

Within the totality of being there may be contained 'glories', 'majesties' and 'powers' of which mankind knows nothing and ever will know nothing. It may be of these that popular devotion is speaking when it speaks of 'a glory of God', 'a majesty of God' or 'a power of God' which transcends the glory, the majesty or the power of the known universe. If this is so, then popular devotion, or the popular expression of devotion, is not seriously misleading. But it becomes misleading if and when it suggests that the totality of what is must be far surpassed by the potentiality which remains, intact and unexpended, in the Creator: when it identifies 'the glory of God', 'the majesty of God' or 'the power of God' with an immeasurable reserve which is held back from, not imparted to, the being of the universe: when it speaks of transcendent glory, majesty or power which may be contrasted with the glory, majesty or power which is imparted to the totality of the creation: when it represents the whole creation as relatively insignificant when measured against the scale of a transcendent God.

The image of the creation suggested by popular devotion is an image of serene and effortless activity – the activity, one might say, 'of the left hand of God'. 'He spake the word and they were made: He commanded and they were created'. 'By the word of the Lord were the heavens made, and all the hosts of them by the breath of His mouth'. Whatever may have been the original intention of such words, they convey an impression of easy control and limited endeavour, of resources held in reserve and power unused. 'The word of the Lord' suggests the very lightest and most effortless expression of the divine will: 'the breath of His mouth' an activity so easy as to be barely perceptible. There is nothing of the giving of self, and therefore nothing of the authenticity of love, in activity so light and easy.

Creation is presented as an almost trivial activity: and its ultimate trivialisation appears not in popular devotion but in that school or fashion of contemporary theology which describes the creation in terms of the activity of 'play'. Here, it would seem, is an almost explicit repudiation of the possibility that the creation is the work of authentic love.

The imagery of popular devotion suggests a divine supremacy over the universe – a supremacy such that whatever may be predicated of the universe in terms of glory, majesty or power may be predicated to a yet higher degree of God. Supremacy is not the relationship of the artist to the work of art, nor of the lover to the object of His love. An artist is not to be described by identifying, and raising to a higher degree, those qualities which are present in his work; nor a lover by seeing him as the beloved 'writ large'. That God should be superior, in every or any respect, to an inferior universe is a quite illegitimate deduction from the doctrine of creation. It is also a deduction which endangers the integrity of religion. For it tends to reduce religion to the prudent recognition of divine supremacy; to suggest that God is to be respected for the superiority of His powers and resources to any challenge or comparison that might be offered; and to make the inferiority of the creature sufficient reason for reverence and worship on the part of the creature. Respect on the part of an inferior may be dictated by prudence: but it can hardly be justified by moral sensitivity. Superiority as such confers no moral right to respect: in particular, superiority of power confers no such right.

The contemporary age has seen more clearly than its precursors the moral ambiguity of power. Through the possession and exercise of ever-increasing power in his own hands, man has discovered the distinction between power and worth, and the irrelevance of the one to the other. The argument that one who is great in power should therefore be respected is seen to involve a non sequitur; and, psychologically, the display of power has become an obstacle rather than an assistance to respect. Power is seen as involving privilege rather than worth: why should the possession of privilege carry a further entitlement to respect? So religious imagery which displays and celebrates the supremacy of divine power neither convinces the head nor moves the heart. It is relevant only to those to whom the practice of religion is a rule of prudence. If the work of God in creation is the work of love, then truth demands an imagery which will do justice to the limitless self-giving which is among the marks of authentic love: and the imagery which the head demands may have a new power of appeal to the moral sensitivity of the heart.

As a parenthesis, we may illustrate the kind of imagery which might express the self-giving of God in creation. A doctor tells of an operation which, as a young student, he observed in a London hospital. 'It was the first time that this particular brain operation had been carried out in this country. It was performed by one of our leading surgeons upon a young man of great promise for whom, after an accident, there seemed to be no other remedy. It was an operation of the greatest delicacy, in which a small error would have had fatal consequences. In the outcome the operation was a triumph: but it involved seven hours of intense and uninterrupted concentration on the part of the surgeon. When it was over, a nurse had to take him by the hand, and lead him from the operating theatre like a blind man or a little child.' This, one might say, is what self-giving is like: such is the likeness of God, wholly given, spent and drained in that sublime self-giving which is the ground and source and origin of the universe.

The activity of God in creation must be precarious. It must proceed by no assured programme. Its progress, like every progress of love, must be an angular progress – in which each step is a precarious step into the unknown; in which each triumph contains a new potential of tragedy, and each tragedy may be redeemed into a wider triumph; in which, for the making of that which is truly an 'other', control is jeopardised, lost, and, through activity yet more intense and vision yet more sublime, regained; in which the divine creativity ever extends and enlarges itself, and in which its endeavour is ever poised upon the brink of failure. If the creation is the work of love, then its shape cannot be predetermined by the Creator, nor its triumph foreknown: it is the realisation of vision, but of vision which is discovered only through its own realisation: and faith in its triumph is neither more nor less than faith in the Creator Himself – faith that He will not cease from His handiwork nor abandon the object of His love. The creation is 'safe' not because it moves by programme towards a predetermined goal but because the same loving creativity is ever exercised upon it.

The existence of evil must be seen as the expression or consequence of the precariousness of the divine creativity. Evil is the moment of control jeopardised and lost; and the redemption of evil is inseparable from the process of creation. This principle is derived from reflection upon the nature and activity of authentic love; and we must guard it against two possible misinterpretations. In the first place, it does not imply a radical dualism. It does not imply that the Creator works upon a 'material' which is fundamentally alien or resistant to the shape which He would impose upon it; nor does it imply a 'power' working to oppose or frustrate the Creator's power. It implies only that that which is created is 'other' than He Who creates; that its possibility is not foreknown but must be discovered; that its possibility must be 'worked out' in the creative process itself; and that the working out must include the correction of the step which has proved a false step, the redemption of the move which, unredeemed, would be tragedy. In artistic creation the artist wills both content and form: neither is fundamentally alien or resistant to that which he would create. The artist chooses, let us say, a certain size of canvas as suitable for a certain theme. But, as he works, this formal requirement, which he himself has willed, imposes a discipline upon his creativity. He is faced with the problem of working within his self-chosen form; and the solution to the problem must be worked out in the creative process. The problem arises not because the artist has chosen the 'wrong' form but because he has chosen *some kind* of form – because he has chosen not merely to express himself but to do so in some kind of determinate way. This problem is present in all creativity, in every process of imparting oneself to that which is truly other than oneself: one must 'find the way' in which, through risk and failure and the redemption of failure, the other may be able to receive.

In the second place, the principle does not imply that evil is willed by the Creator, either for its own sake or as a means to a greater good. The artist does not will the moment of lost control, nor intend it as a means to the completion and the greatness of his work. He does not will the demand which that moment makes upon him – the demand to redeem it and to save his work. He does not will the problem of creativity: his will is to overcome the problem in every particular form and moment in which it may arise. Each problematical moment is unforeseen and unforeseeable: it arises because the object of creation is truly an other. The demand on the artist is to overcome the unforeseeable problem – to handle it in such a way that it becomes a new and unforeseen richness in his work. The artist fails not when he confronts a problem but when he abandons it: and he proves his greatness when he leaves no problem abandoned. Our faith in the Creator is that he leaves no problem abandoned and no evil unredeemed.

We do not believe, of the children who died at Aberfan, that God willed their death as a means to some greater good. If we so believed, we should find that alleged 'good' tainted, compromised and unacceptable: like Ivan Karamazov, we would have no part in it and would 'hand in our ticket'. We believe that, at the moment when the mountain of Aberfan slipped, 'something went wrong': the step of creative risk was the step of disaster: the creative process passed out of control. Our faith is in a Creator Who does not abandon even this, nor those who suffered, wept and died in it, but Who so gives Himself that He finds, for the redeeming of this, yet more to give, and knows no respite until the slag-heap has become a fair hillside, and the hearts of the parents have been enlarged by sorrow, and the children themselves understand and are glad to have so feared and wept and died. Our preaching on the Sunday after the tragedy was not of a God Who, from the top of the mountain, caused or permitted, for His own inscrutable reasons, its disruption and descent; but of One Who received, at the foot of the mountain, its appalling impact, and Who, in the extremity of endeavour, will find yet new resource to restore and to redeem.

The God Who will not abandon and to Whom nothing save Himself is expendable is often misinterpreted in popular devotion as the God of foreordained and programmed purposes. It is assumed that for that to which He gives purpose He already has purpose, and that of that which He uses He has predetermined the use. To make this assumption is to destroy the basis for any real analogy between divine and human creativity, and to exclude from the activity of God all the precariousness and all the poignancy of love. It is to reduce the divine activity to a kind of *production* – a mere drawing out, or display, of that which already is. If the purpose of God in creation is foreknown and foreordained to fulfilment, then the creation itself is vanity. Within it nothing decisive happens, and nothing new: it is merely the unwinding and display of a film already made. On the other hand, to interpret the creation as the work of love is to interpret it as the new, as the coming-to-be of the hitherto unknown, and so as that for which there can be no precedent and no programme. If the creation is the work of love, its 'security' lies not in its conformity to some predetermined plan but in the unsparing love which will not abandon a single fragment of it, and man's assurance must be the assurance not that all that happens is determined by God's plan but that all that happens is encompassed by His love.

The activity of God in creation must be vulnerable. It would be more natural to say that, in His activity, God Himself must be vulnerable, but in saying this there would be a danger of introducing an excess of anthropomorphism into our reflection on the love of God. In our human experience we know the vulnerability of the lover in and through the beloved – a vulnerability in every aspect of his feeling and personality. In and through the beloved a man's pride may be hurt, his wit enlivened, his shyness overcome, his ambition fired, his hope fulfilled. Love exposes the whole range of a man's susceptibility to the power of the beloved: through the beloved he is affected, to a higher degree, in every way in which he is capable of being affected by any person or by any circumstances. If we know a man's susceptibilities, we can predict something of the effect which love will have upon him – the manner in which he will be vulnerable. We can predict that one man will be easily hurt by one whom he loves, and another easily moved to anxiety. But we do not know the susceptibility of God, nor whether it is proper to speak of a God Who may be 'hurt', 'disappointed' or 'made glad'. So if we say that God Himself is vulnerable in and through His creation we hardly know what we are saying. We know that, if the love of God is authentic, God is not 'detached' from His creation. He gives to it 'power of meaning' as well as power of being. But we do not know what this meaning is, nor whether the creation has power to bring joy or grief, delight or distress, to Him Who is its Creator. We should probably feel no impropriety in saying that God 'delights' in His creation, or that He is 'grieved' in the tragic aspects of that to which He gives Himself in love. We should feel it improper to speak of the 'pride' of God in His creation, or of His 'irritation' over its problems. But between that which is properly predicated of God and that which is improperly predicated we cannot draw the line with any confidence, for we do not know the 'susceptibility' of God.

We know only that God is love. We know only the *activity* of God. We know that God is vulnerable only in the sense in which the activity of love may be said to be vulnerable. We have seen in the previous chapter that love is not vulnerable in the sense that it may be diminished or destroyed by that which it loves, or in the sense that love gives to the other the power to determine love's own being. This cannot be so – since it is only through the being of love that the other has any power at all. The power which love gives to the other is power to determine the issue of love – its completion or frustration, its triumph or tragedy. This is the vulnerability of authentic love – that it surrenders to the other power over its own issue, power to determine the triumph or the tragedy of love.

The vulnerability of God means that the issue of His love as triumph or tragedy depends upon His creation. There is given to the creation the power to determine the love of God as either triumphant or tragic love. This power may be called 'power of response': upon the response of the creation the love of God depends for its triumph or its tragedy. In the next chapter we shall reflect upon the response of the creation, and its varieties of level or degree. For the present we must consider more fully what is involved in saying that God depends upon the creation for the issue of His love as triumph or as tragedy.

Man discovers in himself not only the need to be loved but also the need to love. When he loves, and when his love is completed and fulfilled in the response of the beloved, he finds himself the gainer. His life has a richness which was not there before. Certainly man's power to love also contains tragic possibilities: for when his love is rejected or unfulfilled he is exposed to the extremity of anguish and loss. One may say that, because of man's power to love the game of his life is played for higher stakes, and contains greater possibilities both of gain and of loss. But for lower stakes it would perhaps not be worth playing. Therefore, despite the tragic possibilities which the power to love contains, we need both the power to love and the response of the other to our love: and without the satisfaction of this double need we are incomplete.

Christian theology asserts that this 'need' is met within the being of God Himself, and requires, for its satisfaction, no response from the creation. In the dynamic relationship within the being of the Trinity, love is already present, already active, already completed and already triumphant: for the love of the Father meets with the perfect response of the Son. Each, one might say, endlessly enriches the Other: and this rich and dynamic interrelationship is the being and life of the Spirit. Therefore nothing beyond the being of God is necessary to the fullness or fulfilment of God. God is not like man – who must look beyond himself to an other who, by responding, will satisfy his need to love. Within the mystery of the divine being there is present both the power to love and the triumphant issue of love in the response of the Beloved.

Such is the assertion of Trinitarian theology. It precludes

any possibility that the creation has a claim upon the Creator – the claim of being a means to, or necessity for, the divine fulfilment. No creature may cherish the thought that, without him, without his being and his response, God Himself would be reduced or unfulfilled or incomplete. No creature may place his confidence in a relationship of mutual necessity between himself and his Creator. It is not necessary to the being or the fulfilment of God that any creature, or any created thing, should be.

Trinitarian theology asserts that God's love for His creation is not the love that is born of 'emptiness'. It is not analogous to the love with which a woman, deprived of children, may love a dog or a doll. It is the love which overflows from fullness. Its analogue is the love of a family who, united in mutual love, take an orphan into the home. They do so not of need but in the pure spontaneity of their own triumphant love. Nevertheless, in the weeks that follow, the family, once complete in itself, comes to need the new-comer. Without him the circle is now incomplete: his absence now causes anxiety: his waywardness brings concern: his goodness and happiness are necessary to those who have come to love him: upon his response depends the triumph or the tragedy of the family's love. In spontaneous love, the family has surrendered its own fulfilment and placed it, precariously, in the orphan's hands. Love has surrendered its triumphant self-sufficiency and created its own need. This is the supreme illustration of love's self-giving or self-emptying – that it should surrender its fullness and create in itself the emptiness of need. Of such a nature is the Kenosis of God – the self-emptying of Him Who is already in every way fulfilled.

The Kenosis of God means that, for the being of the universe, the being of God is totally expended, without residue and without reserve: expended in endless and precarious endeavour of which the issue, as triumph or

tragedy, has passed from His hands to depend upon the
response which His love receives. That response will not
destroy or diminish His love: but it will mark it as
triumphant or as tragic love. 'Tantus labor non sit cassus' –
may such labour not prove in vain. The prayer which is
moved by reflection upon the work of redemption may be
moved with equal fervour by reflection upon the work of
creation: for in each appears a totality of self-giving for a
work which is ever precarious and ever poised between the
possibilities of triumph and tragedy. Redemption, indeed,
is a part of creation – it is the task of 'winning back' which
is ever-present in the risk of creativity: and the Word of God
by Whom the heavens were made, is that same Word of
God who 'suffered to redeem our loss'. We may say that
Christ, the Incarnate Word, discloses to us, at the climax of
His life, what word it was that God spoke when 'He commanded and they were created'. It was no light or idle word
but the Word of love, in which, for the sake of an other, all
is expended, all jeopardised and all surrendered. The Cross
of Christ discloses to us the poignancy of the creation itself
– the tragic possibility that, when all is given in love, all
may be given in vain.

The Word of God dwelt among us 'full of grace and
truth'. In Him the truth of God is disclosed with
graciousness. He discloses to us, on Good Friday and
Easter Day, both the tragic and the triumphant possibilities
of the love of God. But the disclosure is made graciously;
Easter comes after Good Friday: tragedy is 'swallowed up'
in triumph: and mankind, having seen the tragic possibility, is called away to devote his faith, hope and service to the
possibility of love's triumph. The Word of God discloses to
us at Christmas the helplessness of love at the hands of its
own creatures – the fact that it is in their hands, vulnerable
to their hands, dependent upon their hands for its own
triumphant or tragic issue. But the disclosure is made

graciously, in the form and presence of a Child. The helplessness of a child is a manageable helplessness, about which we know what we may do, by which our heart and our will are touched. It is not a harrowing helplessness, before which one who saw it might stand appalled. The same truth, the tragic possibility of the love of God, might have been exposed to us in harrowing and appalling form.

On a certain night, shortly before Christmas, I stood in the beautiful Church which, in due time, rose beside the commonplace building where, at the first, the people of a new community had worshipped. The Church was ready for Christmas; and the quiet light of candles enhanced its tranquillity and beauty. It was very late: but the beauty of Christmas and of its symbols seemed peculiarly intense that night; and I was glad to receive it while I might. I was disturbed by a noise behind me – a dull thud: and I saw, against the glass door which led into the Church, and no more than a couple of feet from the bottom of the door, a face pressed, and grotesquely distorted by the pressure. A man was half slumped, half kneeling against the door. He was drunk; and when we talked and he gradually became more sober, it was clear that, though he was quite young, he was already an alcoholic. His experience of life was nothing but the experience of conflict and squalor: and at Christmas he expected nothing different. When at last I retired to sleep my mind must have dwelt on the tragic and distorted face which had, so to speak, invaded the beauty of Christmas. For I dreamed: and in my dream a rubbish-collector came to me and told me that he had been clearing up after a riot; and I myself saw the huge pile of stones and cans and waste paper and scrap metal which he had collected. Then the man touched my arm and said, 'But what am I to do? For deep within the pile, buried at the bottom of it, I have seen a living face'. Though my own eyes did not see the face, I knew in my dream that it must be the face of God.

A few hours later, when I preached in Church, I was compelled to speak of my dream. For it seemed to suggest a different way in which the truth of Christmas might have been disclosed – a harrowing and appalling way. It made one newly sensitive to, and grateful for, the graciousness of the way in which the truth of Christmas is in fact disclosed to us. But, in substance, it was the same truth. It was the truth of a God Who, in love, is totally expended for the being of His creation – so that He is helpless under its weight and barely survives for its everlasting support; so that, in the tragedies of the creation, in its waste and rubbish, God Himself is exposed to tragedy: so that the creation is sustained at the cost of the agony of One Who is buried and almost wholly submerged within the depth of it.

Bonhoeffer, in one of his poems, wrote of a God –

'. . . poor and scorned, without shelter or bread
   Whelm'd under weight of the wicked, the weak, the dead . . .'

T. S. Eliot discovered, in the associations of certain images, 'the notion of some infinitely gentle, infinitely suffering thing'. But this kind of imagery, this kind of 'notion', does not belong to conventional representations of the divine creation. Our conventions are still determined to a large degree by the historical roots out of which our faith has grown. Those roots lie in the soil of Judaism, and in the heroic struggle of Judaism to establish and sustain a pure monotheism. The struggle was against the temptation to identify God with any impressive or appealing element within the totality of being – with sun or mountain top, with natural power or animal virility. Great as these things were, the unseen God was greater. The fundamental tenet of monotheism is that God is *qualitatively* different from any element within the whole of nature and from nature as a whole – different as artist is different from artefact, as giver from gift, as that which originates from that which is derived. But this qualitative difference is often expressed in the literature of Judaism in *quantitative* form or metaphor. 'He taketh up the isles as a very little thing'. God is distinguished from nature by quantitative superiority: that which is impressive in nature is represented as yet more impressive in God: the greatness of God belongs to the same parameter as the greatness of nature. One may say that the historic task of monotheistic Judaism was to identify or define the proper Object of religion – to point to the source or ground of being and value, and to distinguish it from everything to which being or value is given. But definition proceeded, in part, by description – by the attribution to God of a quantitative superiority of those powers of which, in nature and in man, He is the source and origin and condition. Definition acquired an accretion or penumbra of description: and the legacy of Judaism was not simply a definition of the Object of religion, of Whom the Incarnate Word might disclose the nature and description, but an imagery which included an element of description – the description of God as quantitatively superior to all the glories, powers and capacities of nature and of man.

This legacy of inherited description appears to have inhibited the reflection of Christianity upon its own description of God as love, and upon the implications of this description. The conventional representation of God is of One by Whom, in the creation, nothing is expended and nothing jeopardised, Who presides serene over the assured unfolding of a predetermined purpose, Whose triumph is assured before His activity begins, and Who, in the appearance of giving, is ever maintaining, intact and unimpaired, His own supremacy. We see in this representation more of benevolence, of condescension, of manipulation and even of possessiveness than of authentic love. We have observed in the previous chapter how human sensitivity is affronted when some lesser thing is offered under the name or guise of love: and we cannot deny that Christiantiy affronts when it presents a divine benevolence or condescension under the name of love. It may well be that the fundamental suspicion which Christianity arouses is directed not against the disparity between its practice and its message, but against that message itself: it may be the suspicion that, when Christianity speaks of the love of God, it means something different from what it says.

If God is love, and if the universe is His creation, then for the being of the universe God is totally expended in precarious endeavour, of which the issue, as triumph or as tragedy, has passed from His hands. For that issue, as triumphant or as tragic, God waits upon the response of His creation. He waits as the artist or as the lover waits, having given all. Where the issue is tragedy, there remains only the unbelievable power of art or love to discover within itself, through the challenge of the tragic, the power which was not there before – the power of yet further endeavour to win back and redeem that which was going astray. Where the issue is triumph, there remains only the will of love to surrender triumphant self-sufficiency in yet larger, more distant, more generous endeavour. Always, for the richness of the creation, God is made poor: and for its fullness God is made empty. Always His helplessness waits upon the response of the creation. To anyone who does not understand this, or cannot accept it, we must answer, 'Nondum considerasti quanti ponderis sit amor, quanti ponderis creatio'.[2]

---

2. You have not yet weighed the cost of love, the cost of creation.'

5. The Response of Being

In every moment and every fragment of the precarious endeavour of creation there exist the twin possibilities of the triumph and the tragedy of love. No two possibilities could be more different. Since love involves a limitless giving, the tragic issue of love means that *all* has been given in vain: the triumphant issue means that *all* has achieved new value in its service to that triumph.

Where an activity is known to be the work of love, it is scarcely possible to be indifferent to its issue. A cause for which others have given their lives makes, for that reason, a certain claim upon our loyalty. A building which has been preserved by the care of centuries is, for that reason, the more worthy of protection. A gift which has been made to us in love is, for that reason, not to be squandered. Our attitude to that cause, that building or that gift may not be wholly determined by our knowledge of the love which has been devoted to it: it may be that our need in the present will justly over-ride our respect for the past. But it is hard to imagine a person in whom such knowledge affected his attitude not at all. In considering the service of a cause or the preservation of a building, we regard such knowledge as a matter of relevance: we expect even a child to know that a gift of love is worthy of care. We rebuke a child for squandering a gift of love: and our rebuke is not simply on the grounds that the giver may learn what has happened and be disappointed, offended or hurt. We point out to the child that the gift is a gift of love; and leave him to draw his own conclusion that it deserves his care.

A child is able to draw this conclusion. Respect or reverence for love appears to be no less universal among mankind than is the need for love. It is the reverse side of that just indignation which rejects the affectation or pretence of love. It is more than respect for the person who loves: it is certainly more than the will not to offend or hurt that person. Though the lover be unknown, or though he be beyond feeling or awareness, we respect his love; and we respect that in which his love has been manifested or for which his love has been given. This respect may be described as the will that love should triumph: it is love of love's triumph and aversion to its tragedy: it is attachment to the cause of love and resentment of that by which love's cause is frustrated or its work made vain. Where love is recognised as love, the two possibilities, of its triumph and of its tragedy, evoke in each man a sharp and even passionate antithesis of attitude. The malevolence that can will love's tragedy and the insensitivity which can be indifferent to its triumph belong to the pathology of humanity.

If the creation be seen as the work of love, then no normal man can be indifferent to that response of the creation on which depends the triumph or the tragedy of love. The problem is to identify that response: to see what it is in the concrete reality of the universe that determines the triumph or the tragedy of the love of God. With this difficult problem the present chapter is concerned.

We have used the phrase 'in the concrete reality of the universe'. The phrase suggests, and is intended to suggest, the stones and trees and stars and men and actions of this or any moment. It might be argued that this is the wrong place, and the wrong level, at which to look for the triumph or tragedy of the love of God. It might be argued that some of the 'things' in this disparate list are merely expendable means for the emergence or support of other and more important 'things': or that all these 'things' are mere preliminaries, inconsequential in themselves, to that final state of the universe in which, and only in which, shall emerge the triumph or the tragedy of the love of God. It might be argued that, in looking at 'the concrete reality of the universe' at any particular place or moment we are looking in the wrong place for the fulfilment or frustration of the purpose of God in creation.

Certainly men have looked in other places. When the universe seemed small and man the undisputed centre of it, the purpose of God was generally believed to be fulfilled in the destiny of the human soul. The drama of the universe was the drama of human salvation – a drama in which stones and trees and stars were no more than the necessary properties or scenic effects. They were the necessary setting for the fulfilment of God's purpose. They were passive instruments, to be manipulated by God and used by man for the support of life and the instruction of the human mind. In themselves they were irrelevant to God's purpose, and could contribute nothing either to its fulfilment or its frustration. The world of nature was no more than the backcloth to the drama of man: and man must not be distracted by it from attention to God's one over-riding purpose – the achievement of human salvation.

An enlarged view of the universe brought with it, inevitably, a larger view of the purpose of God. Reflection on the richness, variety and extent of the universe suggested a hope or vision of 'that far-off divine event towards which the *whole creation* moves'. Theologians of the nineteenth century wrote of 'the consummation of the universe'. The vision was of a future event or state of affairs of such transparent excellence that all that had gone before would be 'justified', or disclosed as purposeful, by that 'end' to which it contributed or which emerged from it. The consummation of the universe would disclose one purpose served in every fragment of its constitution and history. The concrete reality of the present would be discovered, in the future, to have contributed to the building of the future – a future so excellent that the meaning of the present would be made plain and its purpose vindicated. Already, within certain areas of reality, evolutionary theory could show how each lower stage of development was necessary to the emergence of a higher: extrapolation from this theory might explain how every fragment of the universe, through every moment of its history, was necessary to the emergence of that final, self-authenticating excellence which would be both the fulfilment and the disclosure of God's purpose in creation.

The cosmology of the present age no longer gives credibility to this kind of vision. In the universe as a whole it detects no development towards a future condition which will be different in kind from the present. 'The emergence of the higher' may still be detected in the history of life on one planet: but it no longer provides a useful model for the general understanding of the universe. There is no longer reason to suppose that the future condition of the universe will explain or 'justify' the concrete reality of the present; that it will disclose that reality as the necessary means to the fulfilment of a 'higher' and self-authenticating purpose. There is no reason to believe in a future which will contain the key to the meaning and purpose of the present. If there is no purpose to be detected in the concrete and contemporary reality of a particular stone or tree or star, then no purpose will be detected in the total reality of the universe a thousand million years from now. If the triumph or tragedy of the love of God is not to be seen in the concrete reality of the present, there is no reason to suppose that it will be better seen in the reality of the future.

We must walk by the light we have. It is possible that yet further developments in cosmological study may restore the vision of the 'emergence of the higher' or may provide some quite new model for detecting or understanding the pur-

pose of the creation. But for the present we must work with
the model we have – the model of a universe in which
change is towards no particular goal and is in no one direction, and is no more than internal flux and spatial expan-
sion: the model of a universe which points to nothing but
the enlargement in space and time of what it already is.
Therefore the response which determines the triumph or
tragedy of the love of God must be sought by the theologian
in the universe as it is – in the concrete reality of stone or
tree or star or man or action which he himself encounters or
apprehends.

The problem which challenges the theologian is to
detect, in stone or tree or star or man or action, 'power of
response': to define what 'response' or 'power of response'
might mean when predicated of particular things or beings
within the totality of the universe. Dimly we perceive three
possibilities, or three levels, of response: the response of
nature, the response of freedom and the response of
recognition.

The response of nature is that a thing should be that
which it was to be: that, out of the precarious endeavour of
creation, it should 'come right'. If creation be the work o
love, then there is always the possibility that that which is
created may 'come wrong'. That it should 'come right' is
the response in which love becomes triumphant: that it
should 'come wrong' the response in which love becomes
tragic.

But the question arises whether these phrases 'come
right' and 'come wrong' have any meaning when applied to
the concrete realities of the world of nature. The common
understanding of nature is of a system determined in every
detail by 'laws of nature'. Within such a system, no detail
could be other than it is: if the laws are 'right' then every
detail must be 'right': if the laws are 'wrong' then every
detail must be 'wrong'. It is immaterial whether the laws of

nature are conceived to be the work of a Creator or mere facts or forces of unknown origin: if they determine every detail of nature, then no detail can, in any meaningful sense, be either 'right' or 'wrong'. Each detail is neither more nor less than what it must be.

Nevertheless, human sensibility shows an increasing reluctance to accept this conclusion. Man knows himself to be a part of nature: he also knows his capacity to 'spoil' other parts of nature. William Blake knew that 'a robin red-breast in a cage puts all heaven in a rage': and Blake's indignation at the abuse of nature is felt increasingly in the contemporary world. Such indignation presupposes that there is a 'proper' and an 'improper' place for a robin, a tiger or a calf: and that the proper place is not a cage or a broiler house. Each creature is alive in the cage: none is 'suffering' in any way that can be detected or measured: yet we are driven to say that in each case a creature is 'deprived', that it has a 'right' to more space and freedom, that its present condition is a distortion or abuse of nature. In each case a detail of nature is 'wrong'. Whereas a robin preserving its territory or a tiger hunting for prey is 'right', a caged robin or tiger is 'wrong'. It is immaterial that the creature is caged not by 'natural causes' but by the exercise of man's will: for man himself is a part of nature. Within the system of nature something has 'come wrong' when a creature born for freedom exists in a cage.

It can hardly be denied that man is becoming increasingly aware of the 'rights' of other creatures, and of the possibility that the rights of one creature may be transgressed by another, or its place usurped. Along with this awareness has grown the concept of 'the balance of nature'. The model is of a system so delicately balanced that a minor disturbance can have far-reaching consequences, and that the normal oscillation of the system around a central point can erupt into a violent and cataclysmic swing.

The balance of nature may be disturbed by man – himself a part of nature: it may also be disturbed by elements which are yet more obviously within the system – the outbreak of a forest fire, a volcanic eruption or a disease among a certain species. In the normal equilibrium of nature, the forest becomes dry in summer: but if it should become marginally more dry than usual it is exposed to 'chance' – to the spark caused by the impact of a falling stone, or to the effect of the sun's rays on a fragment of mica. Then the forest erupts in flame: a habitat and the life that depends upon it are destroyed: the consequences spread far beyond the boundaries of the forest. Then, in the course of time, life returns to the dead land – tentatively, as it were, at first, in many competing forms and species: eventually new flora and fauna become established, and the equilibrium of nature is restored.

Where the balance of nature is disturbed, nature, and the creativity of nature, is not destroyed. The point of disturbance is not abandoned. The dead forest may become the 'niche' for the emergence of a new species or the habitat of flora and fauna yet richer than before. The point of disturbance has then become a point of new development. It would hardly misrepresent the situation to say that a natural tragedy has been redeemed and turned into triumph.

As, through microscopic study, man becomes ever more aware of the internal complexity and delicacy of nature, he discovers here also a picture of balance, equilibrium and the 'chance' disturbance which is a cataclysm. Within the immense complexity of a cell lies the possibility of the 'chance' mutation through which a creature will become a freak or a man an imbecile: and to see such a creature or such a man is to see the tragedy of nature 'come wrong'. Yet the possibility remains that the tragedy may be redeemed – that the freak may be the point of development of a new and remarkable species, or that the imbecile may be loved as few are loved. If this should come about, then the 'chance' mutation has become a 'challenge' which has been met by a new phase or level of creativity: and it has been redeemed from tragedy to triumph.

We have been describing a certain way of looking at the world of nature. It includes an awareness of the 'rights' of nature, of the equilibrium of nature and of the patient inventiveness of nature. It uses the concept of 'laws of nature', but it interprets these laws not as irresistable and all pervasive 'forces' but rather as statistical generalisations. It bases its own research and study on the normality of things, but it allows the possibility of the 'random variable', of the one case in ten million which, inexplicably, does not conform. Faced with the random variable, it may seek to explain it: it may detect the cause of the freak of nature in the errant or absent chromosome, and may enquire yet further into the cause of such error or absence. But it allows the possibility that its enquiry may end in the sheerly unaccountable, in the exception or variation about which no generalisation can be made, in the case which is 'wrong' according to every conceivable pattern of generalisation. It envisages, as it were, around the fringe of the normal and therefore accountable, a penumbra of 'chance': and though it seeks, by more sophisticated generalisation, to enlarge and extend the limits of the accountable, it remains aware of a shadowy area beyond those limits – the area of the chance factor, the random variable, the ultimately inexplicable fact.

This way of looking at nature permits us to attach some meaning to the concept that the detail of nature may 'come right' or 'come wrong'. Every commonplace detail of nature, every stone or tree, includes an immense richness and variety of lesser detail: in every fragment of it a thousand million lesser fragments cohere and interact. In every fragment of it, therefore, lie one hundred possibilities of 'the one case in ten million' which is abnormal and aberrant, which fits no pattern and cannot be explained: and each of these hundred possibilities contains the threat of a distorted, stunted, diseased or barren tree. Where the threat is actualised, there perhaps stands such a tree; or perhaps there is no tree but only a decaying seed which never germinates; or perhaps out of the unusual distortion of the branches of the tree, a shape has been formed which is strangely beautiful against the winter sky. In the stunted tree we see the tragedy of nature 'come wrong': in the shape on the skyline we see the tragedy of distortion redeemed into the triumph of beauty: in the being of this or any tree we see triumph over the possibility that there might be no tree at all. In the being of the tree we see triumph over the destructive potential of that one case in ten million which is the aberrant step of nature, the point where creativity has gone awry. Where the destructive potential is actualised, we see the tragedy of nature: and we also see, on occasion, that endless inventiveness of nature which, out of the material of tragedy, fashions the possibility of a new kind or level of triumph.

Tentatively, but with growing assurance, theology may interpret the dynamic of nature as the activity of love. Assurance grows with the growing reverence of naturalists themselves for the object and material of their study. Their activity resembles less and less the experimental quest for mastery of a mechanical system. It is informed more and more by the sense that the object of study is not 'expendable' even for the sake of knowledge or in the interests of science. It watches for, and detects, more and more, the inventiveness as opposed to the regularity of nature. Not the fixity of nature but its open-ended creativity informs the attitude of the contemporary naturalist: and if he should attempt to describe in general terms the likeness of that activity which he studies we believe that he could hardly avoid the use of such terms as 'generosity', 'precariousness', 'inventiveness' and 'patience'. The naturalist would, on the whole, use such terms metaphorically: the theologian would use them literally and existentially. But between the modern naturalist's description of the processes of nature and the theologian's description of the creativity of God, there would be a distinct similarity of phrase and tone. Each would know what the other was speaking of. Each could detect, in the concrete detail of the natural world, the reality both of triumph and of tragedy. The theologian will interpret what he detects as a response, within nature, upon which the creative love of God must wait for its issue as triumph or as tragedy. The naturalist may not accept this interpretation, but he will at least understand what it is that the theologian is trying to interpret.

The second possibility, or level, of response to the love of God is the response of freedom. The response of freedom is that a 'thing' should accept that which it was to be. The word 'accept' must be understood as implying the possibility of 'choice': and the word 'choice' implies an awareness of one's own power to choose. Freedom is not merely the power to be or not to be that which one was to be: it includes awareness of that power and of how it may be used.

In nature a 'thing' may or may not 'come right': it may be or not be that which it was to be. This power is vested in it, or given to it, as the work or object of love. At a certain level within nature, the exercise of this power becomes a matter of choice: and within nature as a whole there comes to be an area or enclave of freedom. Normally, though perhaps arbitrarily and even pretentiously, man identifies this area with the area of his own being. Perhaps it is in fact much more extensive: but its extent is irrelevant to the present argument. Man is aware that, within the totality of nature, an enclave exists in which the response to love can be, and indeed must be, the response of freedom.

As we have said, the enclave of freedom may be larger than the area of human existence: but, in another sense, it is clearly smaller. In certain aspects of his being man is no more than a part of nature, and exercises no power of choice. In his physical being, his response to love remains at the level of nature. His physical being, his wholeness and health, may or may not 'come right': but he himself often has little choice in the matter. Yet it is to be remembered that, even at the level of nature at which man has no power of choice, his being may still determine the triumph or tragedy of creative love. In the defect or deformity of a man, though he himself should be unaware of it, appears a tragedy of the creation: and if that which is 'wrong' should be redeemed, there – even though the man himself should still be unaware of it – would appear a triumph. Memory recalls a conversation with a nurse who had worked for over forty years in the same mental hospital, and had come to be in charge of the ward which was the home of the most afflicted patients. 'Most of them', he said, 'do not know night from day, nor where they are, nor who they are'. He explained that few ever had a visitor: that for none could treatment bring any improvement: and that some, apart from the advance of years, were just as they were when first he came to the hospital. But the ward was clean, bright and comfortable; the patients were well and neatly dressed; and, while the nurse talked, his attentive eyes never left his charges, and, from time to time, he moved to one or another to restrain, if he could, some grotesquerie of posture or behaviour, or to assuage some outburst of screams or tears. Questioned about the purpose and motive of his endless care, the nurse said, 'I see it this way. These men are human beings: and human dignity is important: and I do my best to respect and uphold it'. Here, it seemed, though men were below the level of freedom, they were still of value as a part of nature. In them appeared a tragedy of the creation: and though that tragedy could not be raised to triumph by one man's care, it could at least be alleviated, extenuated or lightened.

Man, in his physical being, is simply a part of nature. Yet, even in this aspect, his being is not irrelevant to the tragedy or triumph of creative love. His deformity, defect or indignity is love's tragedy; his wholeness, health and dignity love's triumph.

But man is also capable of the response of freedom. At a certain level of his being, he has the choice of accepting or rejecting 'that which he was to be', the choice of 'coming right' or 'coming wrong'. Normally the choice is exercised in connection with some practical detail of attitude or behaviour; and a man decides by rule of thumb what course of behaviour would be right for him in the circumstances, and what would be wrong. But if he reflects upon his rule of thumb he will normally connect it with some general picture of what he himself 'is supposed to be', of the pattern of behaviour which is fitting and proper to him. So far as he chooses that which in fact is proper to him, his response is the response of freedom and the triumph of the creative love which made him.

In any creative work, the object is discovered in the making of it. Creativity does not proceed by programme or by blueprint: it discovers its goal or objective only as that which is made 'comes right'. What a man 'is supposed to be' emerges only as he himself comes into being. If men are the work of love, no man is made according to a mould or pattern: no man 'comes right' by precisely fitting a mould or conforming to a pattern. But this is not to say that, in the being of a man, 'whatever is is right'; or that 'what a man is supposed to be' is identical with 'that which he chooses to be'. In the practical detail of his life a man is aware of the possibility, determined by his own choice, of 'coming wrong': and one may say in general that a man discovers what he is supposed to be by approximation from his awareness of what he is not supposed to be. In considering the response of nature, we noticed our awareness of the tragic in the world of nature; much more advanced is our awareness of the tragic in the world of man. Interior reflection discloses to us a manifold dis-ease, in which we detect, as interrelated elements, sense of failure, frustration, anxiety, guilt, phantasy – each, in its different way, the awareness of having 'come wrong'. This awareness does not imply that we have a determinate vision of 'what we should be': rather, 'what we should be' is extrapolated from the known unsatisfactoriness of what we are.

This extrapolation is often widened into a statement of what men in general should be: and general principles are sought and taught for the ordering of human life and behaviour. These statements and principles no doubt have their value: but they do not serve as premises from which a man deduces what he should be and therefore the unsatisfactoriness of what he is. He *meets* his own unsatisfactoriness. General principles of life and behaviour serve only as abstract and approximate statements of the shape which a man's life and behaviour would take if his known tragedy were turned into triumph.

Man discovers what he should be by progressive approximation from the known unsatisfactoriness of what he is. This is evident in the individual: it appears also to be true in society. We do not deduce from general principles of what society should be the tragedies of the society in which we live. We encounter those tragedies as tragedies. We know that they should not be. We meet them as a need to be served or as an ill to be remedied. We do not find them 'wrong' because we live by a vision of what society should be: indeed, what is called a 'vision' is often no more than an abstraction – a theoretical statement of what society would be if all such wrongs were righted. The value of such a statement is often doubtful. For example, we meet a sick child whose careless parents have not called the doctor. We know that the situation is wrong and must be put right. We do not deduce the wrongness of the situation from the general principle that the good society cares for the health of all: we see the wrong, and extrapolate from it what would be right. But often, as in the present case, the extrapolation becomes so comprehensive and so vague that it retains no more than an emotive meaning. We know, in a concrete instance, the sickness of a child, the carelessness of parents and the need of a doctor: but through a statement which contains two such ambiguous words as 'care' and 'health' we discover little, if anything, of what 'the good society' would in fact be like.

Therefore, in speaking of the response of freedom to the love of God, we do not find it necessary or possible to describe a general pattern of response – to describe what man, individually or collectively, 'is supposed to be', and what he must be if the divine love is to be triumphant. Such generalisations are apt to be slogans without programmes, principles too vague for any practical applications. Practical experience in the service of the Church discloses, beneath the commonplace and placid surface of life, a remarkable ferment, an endless eruption of 'crises', of points of decision and new possibility. A crisis is a concrete situation of which it may be impossible to say whether the principal elements are psychological, intellectual, social, religious, physical or even financial – of which, indeed, analysis into these various categories may be wholly inappropriate. The crisis is *encountered*. It is suddenly disclosed or deliberately presented by the person who is at the centre of it: and its disclosure or presentation immediately involves the listener, so that he becomes not merely a listener but also a participant. If he maintains a certain detachment as he listens, he adds a further element to the crisis: if he becomes emotionally and argumentatively involved, he adds a different element: if he refuses to listen at all, he adds a third element. The crisis is not necessarily tragic nor pregnant with tragedy. It is sometimes the crisis of new vision or enlarged opportunity. It is not necessarily the eruption of a new situation. It is sometimes the disclosure of a long-cherished dream or a continuing agony. It is a crisis in that the situation may 'go either way' – whether by decision or by force of the circumstances that are involved in it. The situation is one in which various possibilities are taken *seriously*: and its importance lies not in the objective importance of the consequences which may flow from it, but in the seriousness with which one or more people regard those consequences.

To encounter, day by day, this critical ferment in the affairs of men is to become sceptical of the value of general statements of the duty of man and of broad visions of 'the good society' – whether those statements and visions be deduced from theology or from moral or social philosophy. The concrete situation is unique: one understands it only as one enters into it, and by the time one has come to see what 'principles' should be applied to it, one has already affected it. Let us suppose that the crisis is one of despair, where a person appears to be on the verge of suicide. One is not much assisted either by the general principle that suicide is always forbidden, or by the general principle that it is sometimes permissible. For by the time the sufferer can look at the situation objectively, in terms of general principles, the crisis is past. One is guided by the appeal or the offence of the sufferer's despair. This is encountered as a wrong to be righted, a wound to be healed. When the one whose help is sought responds with 'the rule book' – the general statement of principle – his possibility of helping is usually ruled out: for it appears to the sufferer that he has failed to grasp the very core of the situation – which is its uniqueness and individuality. Man in crisis always finds his crisis unique.

Therefore, in the response of freedom, we do not see the advance of man and society towards some predetermined goal – 'the good society', 'the caring society', 'the fulfilment of humanity', 'the emergence of persons as persons'. Our eyes are set upon the concrete and individual crises of human existence, the minute but profoundly serious occasions in which a person, a group of people or a situation between people 'comes right' or 'comes wrong'. In and through such situations we see the angular progress of the ever precarious creativity of the love of God – the risk that fails and must be won back in yet more costly correction, the tragic outcome which must be redeemed, the triumphant outcome which becomes the basis for a yet wider and more generous adventure of love. Man's choice in the endless crises of his existence is the response of freedom – the response upon which love must wait for its triumph or its tragedy. We cannot state in general terms a pattern of response in which appears the triumph of the love of God, nor a pattern in which appears its tragedy: but in the concrete situation of crisis, with its finely balanced possibilities, we can see in which direction triumph lies, and in which direction tragedy. The very seriousness with which we treat the situation is a sign of our recognition of its triumphant or tragic possibilities.

We have detected two levels at which the creature may respond to the Creator, and through its response determine the triumph or tragedy of love. The first is the response of nature, the second the response of freedom. The distinction between the two is not absolute or precise: for many crises are crises both of nature and of freedom. But the distinction is useful in giving meaning to the concept of response. A further distinction, equally useful though still imprecise, may be made between the response of freedom and the third level of response through which love becomes either tragic or triumphant – the response of recognition.

In studying the phenomenology of love, we saw that love is a limitless self-giving. Therefore any particular action or gift of love is no more than a symbol of, or pointer to, that which love aspires to do or give. The action or the gift is one thing: it conveys a certain benefit or possesses a certain intrinsic value. But that to which it points – or, more precisely, that to which love wills it to point – is another and larger thing. If a book is sent to us through the post, it has a certain value – whoever may have sent it and from whatever motive: but if we recognise, from the card enclosed, that it is a gift of friendship and love, it has a larger value. If the card should be lost, we should receive the cash value of the book, or its utility value. But we should not receive its symbolic value. Of that we should be deprived. We should receive the full value of the book only if we recognised it as the gift of love. It is the intention of the giver that, for our own sake, we should recognise the book for what it is: if, through the loss of the card, we fail to do so, his intention is not fulfilled nor his work completed: the fullness of what he would give has failed to reach us. The fullness will arrive only when, through the symbol of the gift, love itself is recognised and received.

Distorted forms of love *demand* from the other the response of recognition. That which they give is given obtrusively, so that the receiver is almost compelled to respond. Rightly, we condemn this parody of love as a kind of blackmail. We suspect that the gift has been made only for the sake of the response which it must elicit: that the giver was not disinterested: and that his affectation of love was simply a means to self-satisfaction or self-aggrandisement. Authentic love, we feel, must be unobtrusive and self-effacing in its methods: it must be disinterested in its motives:

it must be without concern for recognition, gratitude or any other kind of response. We feel that authentic love must work so silently and secretly that, when its benefits are received, it will not be known from where or from whom they come.

Thus a problem arises. Does authentic love seek recognition of itself as love? Its total difference from the love which 'blackmails' suggests that it does not, and that where recognition is sought the authenticity of love is denied. But on the other hand, as we have seen, where love goes unrecognised it cannot complete the fullness of its work. Perhaps we may say that love *needs*, though it does not *seek*, recognition: that it needs, for the completion of its work and for the good of the other, a recognition which it will by no means demand or compel: that it works unobtrusively and yet, for the sake of the other, allows the possibility that it will be recognised. When it is so recognised, when the other has grasped the meaning of its gifts and recognised them as symbols of love, then the work of love achieves its triumphant completion of self-giving.

The recognition of love is not to be thought of as a single, simple and decisive psychological event. It is not like the recognition of a face in a photograph or the recognition in a passing figure of an old acquaintance. It is more akin to the recognition of the quality of a painting, of the significance of an historical event or of the meaning of a poem. It is not borne in upon one irresistibly, in a flash; it comes of the free exercise of attention, discrimination and reflection. The recognition of love, like the recognition of the quality of a painting, is a blessing. It is a blessing which is made possible by the presence of love but which is only received in one's discernment of that presence. We have referred in an earlier chapter to the universal power of discrimination between the authenticity of love and its falsity. This is the power of knowing that a certain 'mark' – for instance, the mark of detachment – is a mark of falsity. One who sees this mark, or believes himself to see it, is convinced that love is false. But the question arises whether he has seen right. An adult will often come to see what he did not see as a child – that the apparent detachment of his parents was affected for his own good, or that, in seeming to control him, they were in fact enlarging his freedom. The recognition by a person of his parents' love often comes gradually – through experience, attention and reflection. It is made possible by his parents' love, but it is achieved only through his own understanding. It is only through his own understanding that the blessing of his parents' love reaches him in its fullness.

So it is with the creative love of God. For the completion of its work, and therefore for its own triumph, it must wait upon the understanding of those who receive it. The love of God must wait for the recognition of those who have power to recognise. Within a certain enclave of reality, recognition or the absence of recognition determines the triumph or the tragedy of love.

A work of art creates the possibility of what we may call a responsive creativity. To recognise its quality, a man must, in some sense, order and articulate the impression which it makes upon him. Great art has a greater blessing to give than a vague impression of its greatness. Its greatness, and therefore its greatest blessing, is received only through the articulation of its greatness – only, that is to say, in responsive creativity. Responsive creativity may, at its best, bear all the marks of original creativity: it may respond to original creativity as Keats responded to Chapman's version of Homer, as Wordsworth to the architecture of King's College Chapel in Cambridge or as Sir John Barbirolli to the works of Mahler. We may say that responsive creativity celebrates original creativity: and this celebration is itself a work of art. Its coming-to-be involves all the dedication and precariousness of original creativity, the same tension between form and content, the same unprogrammed advance, the same possibility of 'coming right' or 'coming wrong'. Responsive creativity finds what it has to say only through the saying of it, and discovers the greatness of what it celebrates only through the celebration of it. Responsive creativity is the coming-to-be one's of own recognition of the blessing conferred by original creativity.

So is is that the love of God, in waiting upon the response of recognition, waits upon its own celebration. It waits upon the response in which its own nature and quality is understood: and this response must not be interpreted as a mere 'state of mind', an impression stamped upon passive material by love's own will. It is not so that greatness in creativity is recognised or understood. The understanding of it is itself a form of creativity – an attempt to articulate, an activity of struggle between the richness of content and the discipline of form, the coming-to-be of that which was not there before. Recognition of the love of God involves, as it were, the forging of an offering: the offering is the coming-to-be of understanding: only where this understanding has come to be has love conveyed its richest blessing and completed its work in triumph. Where understanding is possible but absent, or where it is confused and inarticulate, love's work is incomplete and its issue tragic.

Thus we may say that the creativity of God is dependent, for the completion and triumph of its work, upon the emergence of a responsive creativity – the creativity of recognition. Recognition is to be understood neither as a single psychological event nor as a state of mind brought about by such an event. It is to be understood as creativity directly and explicity responsive to the creativity of God. We may say that the response of recognition *celebrates* the love of God. The final triumph of the love of God is the celebration of His love within that universe which has received that love.

That by which, or in which, the love of God is celebrated may be called 'the Church'. The Church occupies the enclave of recognition within the area of freedom: it is all within the area of freedom which would not be if the love of God were not recognised as love: it is all that is done to articulate awareness of the Creator's love. So defined, the Church is much wider than any recognised ecclesiastical structure, and wider than the sum of all such structures. For it must include the simplest action which is done out of awareness of God's love and the most private meditation which seeks, in unspoken words, to articulate that awareness. But, on the other hand, the Church, even when so defined, is not wholly without structure and without form. For the Church is, or consists of, creative activity: and creative activity, however simple or flexible in form, is never without form. Even in the silence of private meditation there is the endeavour to give shape to awareness, to fix its transience or order its abundance by the discipline of form: and every action, even of the simplest kind, is itself the form in which the vagueness of intention is crystallised into creation. Therefore the Church, so far from being without structure or form, is the sum of all the structures and forms within which men express their recognition of the love of God: and always the being of the Church involves the elements of search and struggle, the dynamic and dialectical encounter between content and form, which is the fundamental characteristic of all creative activity. The Church, however broadly defined, is never pure spontaneity and never free from the discipline of form. Old forms may be abandoned and new forms sought, but so long as the Church is responsive creativity it can never pass beyond the need for form nor escape from the demands of form. In the Church, as in all creative activity, the demands of form, when first encountered, must appear as restriction: only when they are met are they discovered to be liberation.

In the following chapter we shall reflect in more detail upon the meaning of the Church. The present and previous chapters have been concerned with establishing a context within which the word 'meaning' may itself *have meaning*. The conviction in which this essay originated was the conviction that the Church has a meaning which is not reducible, directly or indirectly, to its meaning to human well-being or to any other human goal. But the Church, whatever else it is, is a fragment of material reality: and its power of meaning must be related in some way to the meaning which may be detected in material reality in general. It would be absurd to say that, in the totality of being, the Church alone has meaning. It may have a specific meaning: but this specific meaning must be related in some way to a more general meaning, or power of meaning, which is to be detected throughout the universe in general. We have detected this general power of meaning through the concept of being as 'response'. We have taken seriously the concept that 'to be' is to be created in love: and we have seen that the activity of love includes a *waiting upon* the issue of its activity – a *waiting for* the issue as triumph or tragedy. That which is waited for may be called 'response'. The meaning of all that is lies in its power of response – its power to determine the issue of love as triumph or tragedy. We have detected three levels of the power of response: the power to be (or not to be) that which one was to be: the power to accept (or not to accept) that which one was to be: the power to recognise (or not to recognise) that which one was to be. We have identified the Church with response – or, more strictly, with positive response – at the third level. The meaning of the Church is that in its being creative love achieves the triumphant completion of its work in being recognised as love. Therefore upon the being or non-being of the Church depends the final triumph or tragedy of love – the triumph of being known as love, the tragedy of remaining unknown.

The meaning of being in general is that it determines the triumph or the tragedy of love. The meaning of the Church is that it determines triumph or tragedy at one specific level. The peculiar privilege and burden of the Church is that, in recognising itself and all the universe as the work of love, it recognises what it is that, at every level, is emerging as tragic or triumphant. That which is so emerging is love. The Church recognises what it is that, in the response of being, is poised between triumph and tragedy. It therefore recognises the poignancy of what is happening. It knows that love is not measured outlay from immeasureable resources, nor effortless control of predetermined programme, nor impassive observation of inevitable achievement. It knows that love involves limitless and unreserved expense, precarious endeavour and final helplessness to determine its own issue. That issue is surrendered into other hands. It is the peculiar privilege and burden of the Church that it knows what it is that is surrendered into other hands – that it knows what is happening in the response of nature, the response of freedom and the response of recognition. The Church is what man is and does when he recognises what is happening in the being of the universe.

6. The Offering of the Church

The Church occupies the enclave of recognition: and this enclave belongs within the area of freedom. The Church is an activity and product of freedom. We must exclude from the Church everything which, though 'religious' in form, is not the activity or the product of freedom. Nothing belongs to the Church simply by virtue of its form. Enforced conformity adds nothing to the being of the Church.

All that belongs to the Church belongs also to nature and to freedom. All has power of response at the level of nature and of freedom as well as at the level of recognition. The tragedy of a crippled man remains a tragedy of nature even when that man recognises the love of God: and his healing would be a triumph of love at the level of nature even though love is already triumphant in the man at the level of recognition. The tragedy of talents unused remains a tragedy at the level of freedom even when those talents that are used are used within the Church: and the wider use of talents would be a triumph of love at the level of freedom even if it should contribute nothing to the being of the Church.

Man in the Church belongs also to nature and to freedom; and he may respond to the love of God at the level of nature and of freedom as well as at the level of recognition. Furthermore, inasmuch as he recognises, at every level of response, the triumph or the tragedy of love, he must strive more earnestly, at every level of response, to further love's triumph and to redeem its tragedy. He must use his freedom in the *cause* of love as well as in the *celebration* of love. Indeed his celebration of love may well take the form of more earnest service in the cause of love. Because he recognises the love of God, he may devote himself to the triumph of love in some fragment of the world of nature or some area of human life and society; and, in doing so, he may stand alongside others who do not recognise the love of God, and whose motive is simply that nature or society may 'come right'. His recognition of the love of God may be outwardly indistinguishable from a generous 'care' for the world of nature and human society which surround him.

It is theoretically possible that, in such care, the whole of man's freedom might be absorbed. In circumstances of extreme tragedy, a man might be confronted by endless 'crises' in which love's tragedy might be redeemed or its triumph won. His freedom might be wholly expended in the service which these crises called for: and his recognition of love could then take no other form than service in the cause of love. In such circumstances he would indeed be celebrating the love of God; but his celebration would be indistinguishable in form from the service of another man who, knowing nothing of the love of God, was simply affronted and challenged by the 'wrongness' of the circumstances. In his activity the Church would be present but concealed: it could not be distinguished from, or within, the response of freedom to the demand of circumstances.

It might be argued that such circumstances are not only possible in theory but ever-present in practice: that man lives in a tragic environment, and that he is called to spend all his energies for the redemption or alleviation of tragedy. Evidence could be produced of the evils which stalk the face of the earth – hunger and homelessness, oppression and disease, grief and loneliness. Surely, it might be argued, these constitute a tragic environment, and it is in the redemption of these that the love of God must be celebrated. While these exist, there is no place for any other form of celebration. So long as men weep and grieve and hunger, the proper activity of the Church is identical with, and an indistinguishable part of, the response of freedom to the tragedies of existence.

So it might be argued. But in the concrete reality of existence man is aware of triumph as well as tragedy. There is a time to laugh as well as a time to weep. Though many are hungry many also are fed. Though many are homeless many are happy in their homes. The reality of triumph in one situation is not denied by the reality of tragedy in another: nor can the joy and strength of triumph always be expended in the redemption of tragedy. Sometimes triumph can be so expended – as when the joy of a happy home is put at risk in order that a homeless family may share it, or when a man jeopardises his own strength in the care of an invalid. But the possibilities of freedom are limited: and often there is no way in which triumph can serve to redeem or alleviate tragedy. It is a mere affectation of sensitivity when a man claims that, so long as there is tragedy anywhere in the world, he himself can feel no joy; or that, so long as there is redemptive work, however distant, to be done, he himself will know no rest. In many a concrete situation there is something to spare of triumph and of joy which cannot possibly be expended for the redeeming of tragedy: there is a measure of freedom, of 'leisure', which is unchallenged by the needs and distresses of the surrounding world. Realistically seen, the life of the most 'dedicated' man contains a measure of such freedom: the life of most men contains huge areas of it.

Within this area of freedom lies the possibility of, and necessity for, a distinctive activity of recognition. Here the Church is called into being as a visible and identifiable reality. The recognition of love, which is concealed in redemptive activity at the points of love's tragedy, becomes open celebration at the points of love's triumph: the Church, hidden in service where man has need, celebrates love openly where that need is met. When a man lay wounded on the road between Jerusalem and Jericho, the Church was present but concealed in the person of the Good Samaritan: when ten lepers had been cleansed, the Church was present and identifiable in one who returned 'to give glory to God'. In the nine other lepers who were cleansed love passed unrecognised. Love, triumphant in healing, was exposed to the further possibility of triumph or tragedy at the level of recognition: and in the case of nine men out of the ten this possibility emerged as tragedy. Where the Church might be but fails to be, there the issue of love is tragedy. Where freedom is available for the articulation of responsive creativity, and where that creativity fails to appear as a concrete and visible reality, there the issue of love is tragedy.

In the visible Church man is aspiring to create something which expresses his recognition of the love of God. His creativity is *responsive*: it aspires to be *appropriate to* that which it recognises. Since that which it recognises is love, it aspires to be a loving creativity – a kind of gift or offering. In the visible Church man aspires to make an offering to God: he brings something into being, or sustains something in being, as an offering to God. His offering is the symbol of responsive love. No symbol can adequately convey the limitlessness of love: yet one symbol may be less inadequate than another. The Widow's Mite was a less inadequate symbol than the measured benefactions of the rich. One symbol may express less inadequately than another the unsparingness, the risk or the care that are among the marks of love. As we have already said, the Church is not to be identified with ecclesiastical structure: it includes the simple gesture or the muttered prayer in which, in his privacy, a man recognises his blessedness. But the easy symbol, achieved without cost or effort or attention, is, to that extent, an inadequate symbol. Where the activity of the Church scarcely rises above the level of mere spontaneity, it is inadequate as an expression of responsive love. The proper symbolism of the Church must be achieved at some cost and even at some risk.

Therefore man in the Church is aware of himself as being under a degree of discipline. His aspiration is not to express *himself* but to express responsive love. Therefore he may not use whatever form or symbol comes most naturally to himself and is least demanding upon himself. He must use a form or symbol whose achievement makes upon him some degree of demand and involves him in some kind of cost. Within the Church, he must surrender something of his own freedom and spontaneity: he must bring his life within a form which is not entirely natural to him and not specifically adapted to his own particular temperament and needs. He must see the form of the Church as, in some degree, alien to himself, as that to which he must bring himself to conform. His sense that the Church is alien to him must be overcome not by the changing of the Church but by the changing of himself.

The Church presents itself to man as an institution with a history. It is something which the present inherits from the past, and of which the form is already given. To repudiate form simply because it is no longer 'natural' would be to refuse that surrender of one's own freedom and spontaneity which is involved in authentic love. But, on the other hand, the form of the Church is itself the product of history, and has been determined, at least in part, by the attitudes and presuppositions of other ages. It may be that a form which disciplines the response of one age distorts or destroys the response of another: that a form has come to have such associations that it can no longer express what man would say, but only distort or destroy it. The need then arises for reform. But the reform of the Church is a matter of extreme delicacy and difficulty. For the search is not for the form which will most easily contain the spontaneity of the present age, but for a form which will impose upon that spontaneity a degree of discipline. The task is not simply to bring the spontaneity of the present age within the Church: it is to form that spontaneity into the costly offering of love. Reform of the Church requires more than sociological insight into contemporary trends and attitudes: it requires also the artist's understanding and the lover's experience of the costly discipline of love.

Within the form of the Church, inherited or re-formed, man aspires to present an offering of love – an offering fashioned by discipline out of freedom. This offering is brought into being. It is something that actually is. It belongs to the same level of concrete actuality as the stones and trees and stars in which the creativity of God is expressed and completed. As the creativity of the artist is nothing until, through stuggle and discipline, it discovers itself in the emergence of a work of art, so the responsive creativity of man to the love of God is nothing until it discovers itself in the emergence of the concrete actuality of the Church. The Church is not 'the cause which the Church serves' or 'the spirit in which the Church lives': the Church is the service of that cause and the actualisation of that spirit in words spoken, in bodies in a certain place or posture, in feet walking up a certain hill: in stone placed upon stone to build a Church, in wood carved into the fashion of a Cross: in music composed or practised, played or sung: in the doing of certain things upon a particular day and the giving up of certain things during a particular season: in the fashioning, out of time and care and skill, of something beautiful, and in the maintaining, out of time and care and labour, of the beauty of it: in the gathering and training of others so that they may contribute to and continue and enlarge the offering: in the going out to others so that they may share the offering: in the struggle of brain and pen to find expression and interpretation for the love of God: in the event of worship which celebrates the love of God: in hands stretched out for the receiving of Bread and in lips raised for the touch of Wine. Here, at this level of concrete actuality is the response of recognition to the love of God: here is the work of art, the offering of love, which is the Church.

The understanding of the Church as offering throws fresh light on some of those duties of Churchmanship which are felt rather than understood, and which are performed with diligence but not explained with clarity. It throws light, for example, on that attachment to the Church building itself which obstructs many proposals for reform and reorganisation of the Church. The obstructive fact is that the building is felt to be neither a necessity nor a facility but an offering. Love has been expended upon it and expressed in the care of it. In that love and care the building has been offered to God. That the building is little used, and in that sense unnecessary, is irrelevant. That a similar building stands at no great distance away is also irrelevant. The presentation of such facts as if they were decisive is often, and understandably, resented. Attachment to a Church building is by no means to be dismissed as sentimentality: it may well contain a profound, though possibly inarticulate, understanding of what that building is. In the last analysis, the only justification for the destruction of an offering is that it may become the basis or material of a richer, more lasting or more appropriate offering. This must be the principle which distinguishes the reorganisation of the Church from its destruction.

The understanding of the Church as offering throws light also on the Church's activity of prayer, and especially of intercessory prayer. Intercession is felt to be appropriate, and, indeed, to be a duty: yet on certain interpretations of the activity of God and of the nature of the Church, it is a duty which cannot easily be explained or justified. If the purpose of God proceeds by assured progamme, and if the Church is no more than an instrument for the performance of that programme, intercession can effect nothing and can be no more than an expression of resignation. If, on the other hand, the activity of God is precarious creativity, ever poised between tragedy and triumph, ever redeeming tragedy into triumph; and if the Church is responsive offering to God; then the intercession of the Church is the offering of its will to participate, to uphold, to support. We are moved to intercession by tragedy or the possibility of tragedy: by that which has 'come wrong' or is in danger of 'coming wrong'. We presuppose that this is the situation in which the activity of love will be strained to the greatest intensity, in which love can discover yet further resources only because it must. We are as men watching the most precarious stage of a rescue or a mountain climb, or the supreme effort of an artist or athlete. We have no power to give practical help: he who struggles must struggle in his own strength. Yet the will to help and uphold is strong in us. It demands expression: and it finds expression in the movement of our lips and the involuntary tension of our own limbs. The will is stirred in us by our perception of the peculiar intensity of another's effort: it is to his endeavour, even more than to his cause, that our will responds. Where the progress of his cause is relatively easy, we who watch relax: it is when he is strained and spent that out will is stirred. We are moved to intercession to the degree that, at the point of tragedy or potential tragedy, we understand the intensity of the divine self-giving: and if our intercession is feeble or infrequent, it is because of the feebleness or failure of our understanding. We are assisted in prayer by imaginative sympathy with the person for whom we pray or the situation about which we pray: we are assisted yet more by understanding of that divine activity which is expended upon that person or that situation, of the extremity and costliness of its endeavour. The intercession of the Church expresses our understanding of how costly a thing we are asking when we say 'Thy will be done'.

Another activity which is illuminated by the understanding of the Church as offering is the problematical activity of preaching. Preaching is not always or to all preachers problematical: to some preachers on all occasions, and to all preachers on some occasions, its purpose is plain and its value unquestionable. But to some preachers who preach regularly and over a long period to virtually the same people: who find themselves with little to say that they have not said before: who are doubtful of their own ability to expound and of their own right to exhort: and who detect, among those who have heard, little remembrance of what they have said, and less effect: to such preachers the purpose and value of this time-consuming activity becomes a problem. They feel a duty of preaching, and a failure of duty in failing to preach: but they find it a duty hard to explain or justify. Therefore they may settle for the compromise of continuing to preach but at a lesser expenditure of care and time, and of doing badly that which they can see no adequate reason for doing at all.

If the Church is offering, then the activity of preaching may, on certain occasions, be offering. It may be the offering of ordered thought. As the music of worship is the offering of ordered sound, so preaching may be the offering of ordered thought. It will be the ordering of thought which, in a certain sense, is already present – which is present, on the one hand, in the content of scriptural reading and prayer which is included in a particular act of worship; and, on the other hand, in the minds of those who come to worship. The thought which is to be ordered is, to a certain degree and in normal circumstances, known beforehand to the preacher. He knows, by his own choice or by the rules of a liturgical calendar, what scripture shall be read in worship, what prayers offered, what hymns sung. He also knows, through his own experience, something of 'what people are thinking' on this particular day and in this particular place. His knowledge of the second is, admittedly, imprecise: but if he knows well those among whom he is preaching, he will know something of general attitudes, interests and pre-suppositions. From this he will understand something of the impact of contemporary events – of a national crisis or a local festival, of the closure of a factory in the district or the opening of a park, of an epidemic of sickness or an outbreak of vandalism, of the approach of holidays or the arrival of spring. Through his own sensitivity, experience and reflection, he will know something of what, on a particular day, is 'on people's minds'.

Out of material which is already present, the preacher may fashion an offering of thought to God. He may fashion, out of what scripture says on this day, and out of what people are thinking on this day, a particularised expression of gratitude to God, or wonder, or penitence. His offering is his own in the sense that he has fashioned it: but he has fashioned it, in part, out of material that is already present in those who hear. If he has fashioned the offering well, it will become the offering also of those who hear: its relevance will be recognised and its truth received: the truth of the preacher will become the truth of the hearers also: his thought, ordered into shape acceptable to God, will order the thought also of those who hear, and will create or become a common offering– the best thought of which, on a particular day, particular people are capable. As the music of worship is the best offering that can be made out of various voices, so the sermon may be also an anthem – the best offering that can be made of a variety of thought.

As the musical anthem has done its work when it has been sung, so the sermon has done its work when it has been preached and offered. The preacher, having prepared it with the greatest care, will now destroy the script or erase it from his memory: for the occasion of this particular offering will not recur, and if the same sermon should be preached again there would then be no cost involved in it, and therefore no offering. That the sermon will soon be forgotten by the hearers and even by the preacher is to be expected and not regretted: for if the sermon was intended as offering, and if it was the best of which the preacher was capable, then, in the offering of it, its purpose was achieved and its work completed.

When the Church is understood as offering, it presents, both to those who share its life and to those who observe it, a powerful objectivity. It appears as transcending in meaning and purpose their own subjectivity – as a cause beyond themselves to be served with care and dedication. It appears also as a common cause, to which all may contribute and which none may appropriate; to which each may bring his particular talent and of which none may usurp and monopolise the benefit. It appears as something which all may live for. The Church falls far short of what it should be: and in any particular district it is usually a very small and imperfect offering. Yet, imperfect thought it is, its professed objectivity, its aspiration to be an offering, may have considerable social value and importance. Still the Church contributes to many districts benefits which no social agency designed to meet the needs of man is likely to confer – the intangible benefits of stability, sense of identity, a cause to be served, a meaningful basis for community.

A decade ago the Church – whether because of its traditional structure or because of its understanding of its own role – seemed to many thoughtful people to be socially irrelevant. Some of its own leaders attempted to teach it a new and relevant role, and tortured the structures of the Church into the service of that role. Others abandoned their leadership of the Church to serve the cause of God in ways which seemed more relevant to the needs of contemporary man. Few detached observers of the Church regarded it as of any social significance in an urban environment or as possessing any social influence when compared with the massive agencies of education, health and welfare supported by the modern state.

More recently, however, a certain change of opinion has become apparent. In the first place, some disillusionment has grown up over the effectiveness, or at least the cost-effectiveness, of large scale and highly-structured agencies of social welfare: and individuals within these agencies find themselves at least as frustrated in their will to give practical service to the needs of man as ever Church leaders were frustrated by the structures and attitudes of the Church. In the second place, awareness that we live in a pluralist society has led to a new sensitivity to the variety of human needs, and to the necessity for agencies of many different kinds to meet those needs. That the Church has a 'place' in serving the special needs of a certain section of the community would be more generally recognised now than a decade ago. In the third place, it has been noticed that, whether by the accidents of history or by the nature of its own self-understanding, the Church already possesses certain qualities which most other social agencies aspire with difficulty, and perhaps in vain, to achieve. For example, the Church is locally based: it works as a community: and, as we have already noticed, it points people to a cause and purpose beyond, and greater than, themselves. The possession of these qualities may enable the Church to exert a social influence much greater than its resources of manpower, money and expertise would suggest. It would not be unreasonable to claim that the Church, in understanding itself as the articulation and offering to God of whatever gratitude and responsive love a district may contain, is still performing an important and even irreplaceable service to the well-being of man.

But it is not for this service that the Church lives, nor in this service that it makes its offering. The Church offers itself to the triumph of the love of God – at that particular level of triumph which appears when love is recognised as love, and the final seal is put upon its work. The Church lives at the point where the love of God is exposed to its final possibility of triumph or tragedy – the triumph of being recognised as love, the tragedy of so passing unrecognised that the final gift, the gift of which all other gifts are symbols, the gift of love itself, is never known. The Church cannot endure that this tragedy should be: for it recognises – and this accounts for its existence – what the love of God is. It recognises what it is upon which its own being, and the being of all men, and the being of the universe depend. It is no lightly spoken word of God, no easy gesture, no measured outlay from immeasurable store. It is no controlled unfolding of a predetermined purpose according to an assured programme· it is no manipulation of insignificant objects, predestined to be what they are, wholly dependent, without power of meaning. That upon which all being depends is love expended in self-giving, wholly expended, without residue or reserve, drained, exhausted, spent: love expended in precarious endeavour, ever poised upon the brink of failure, ever questing, ever venturing, ever at the end of its strength yet ever finding, in the challenge of tragedy, yet new strength to redeem that tragedy and restore again the possibility of triumph: love waiting in the end, helpless before that which it loves, for the response which shall be its tragedy or its triumph. To Him Who so waits the Church, with love and shame, presents its tarnished offering – of which may He accept, as a most humble part, the words here written for His sake.

A Hymn to the Creator

Morning glory, starlit sky,
Leaves in springtime, swallows' flight,
Autumn gales, tremendous seas,
Sounds and scents of summer night;

Soaring music, tow'ring words,
Art's perfection, scholar's truth,
Joy supreme of human love,
Memory's treasure, grace of youth;

Open, Lord, are these, Thy gifts,
Gifts of love to mind and sense;
Hidden is love's agony,
Love's endeavour, love's expense.

Love that gives gives ever more,
Gives with zeal, with eager hands,
Spares not, keeps not, all outpours,
Ventures all, its all expends.

Drained is love in making full;
Bound in setting others free;
Poor in making many rich;
Weak in giving power to be.

Therefore He Who Thee reveals
Hangs, O Father, on that Tree

Helpless; and the nails and thorns
Tell of what Thy love must be.

Thou art God; no monarch Thou
Thron'd in easy state to reign;
Thou art God, Whose arms of love
Aching, spent, the world sustain.